OFFICIAL GUIDE
TO THE

NATIONAL MUSEUM

OF

NATURAL HISTORY/

NATIONAL MUSEUM OF MAN

The National Museum of Natural History building, with its Roman-style dome, first opened its doors to the public in 1910.

OFFICIAL GUIDE
TO THE

NATIONAL MUSEUM

OF

NATURAL HISTORY/

NATIONAL MUSEUM OF MAN

Published for the National Museum of Natural History/
National Museum of Man

by the
Smithsonian Institution Press
Washington, D.C.

Printed in Singapore.

Second edition with a new foreword, 1989; revised 1994.

Library of Congress Cataloging-in-Publication Data

Guidebook to the National Museum of Natural History.

1. National Museum of Natural History—Guide-books.
I. National Museum of Natural History (U.S.) II. Title, QH70.U62W2735 1988
508'.074'0153
87-600338
ISBN 0-87474-681-7

9 8 7 6 5 4 3 2
00 99 98 97

Guidebook Staff
Nan Smith, *Writer*
Sharon Barry, *Editor, 1994 Edition*
Chip Clark, *Photographer*
Ruth O. Selig, *Project Coordinator*

Book Development Division Staff, Smithsonian Institution Press
Caroline Newman, *Executive Editor*
Paula Dailey, *Senior Picture Editor*
Heidi M. Lumberg, *Editor*

The following are among the many individuals who provided invaluable assistance in the preparation of this guidebook: Mary Jo Arnoldi, Dan Appleman, Tom Bowman, Alison Brooks, Fred Collier, Bob Emry, John Ewers, Bob Fudali, Laura Greenberg, Charles Handley, Tom Harney, Robert Hoffmann, Nick Hotton, Fran Hueber, Madeleine Jacobs, Adrienne Kaeppler, Ivan Karp, Joan Madden, Betty Meggers, Bill Merrill, Laura McKie, Don Ortner, Raymond Rye, Stan Shetler, Tom Simkin, Paul Taylor, Sven Thomas, Kenneth Towe, Gus Van Beek, Sue Voss, John White, George Zug, Dick Zusi.

The National Museum of Natural History/National Museum of Man would like to thank the Women's Committee of the National Associate Program for their contribution to the guidebook project.

Cover photo: An African bush elephant—the largest land animal of modern times and the Museum's symbol—provides an unusual centerpiece for the Rotunda.

CONTENTS

WELCOME TO THE NATIONAL MUSEUM OF NATURAL HISTORY / NATIONAL MUSEUM OF MAN

Step into this Museum, and you enter the world of nature. There are wonders from all over the globe, and examples of the many varied cultures of humankind. The National Museum of Natural History/National Museum of Man is the oldest and largest of the Smithsonian Institution's 16 museums. The Museum houses the world's richest collection of artifacts and natural objects, including such treasures as the Hope Diamond, fossil dinosaurs, meteorites from space, a life-sized blue whale, a hall of living insects, a living coral reef, stone tools made by our early ancestors, riches from the pharaohs of ancient Egypt, and much, much more. As you look around, we hope you will be fascinated, amazed, delighted, surprised, and informed by the many exhibits, both permanent and temporary.

The story told in these halls is the story of our planet. Its beginnings are wild and fiery, but after the earliest life forms appeared, it was transformed over the next three thousand million years by a marvelous web of evolving living things. Then our own species evolved a mere sneeze ago in our planet's history. But in a brief span *Homo sapiens* has developed cultures of tremendous complexity and richness, many of which are explored in our exhibits. Of course the story has many twists and turns. With the power gained from our ability to harness energy in different forms, we now face the challenge of a new relationship with our beautiful planet. Art and artifact, and the tens of thousands of mineral, vegetable, and animal specimens in our halls all help tell this wondrous and complex story.

But the specimens you see are a minute fraction of the Museum's collections. Behind the scenes a large group of scientists and technical staff care for and study the other 99 percent of this huge collection, researching many aspects of different cultures, past and present, their artifacts, linguistics, music, and folklore. They study biological diversity and evolution, tropical floras and faunas, coral reefs, volcanoes and earthquakes, and the nature of crystals and meteorites from space. I should have said that they are *your* collections, for the 120 million specimens here are held in trust for the nation, and in fact for the world, and they are used by scientists and scholars from around the globe.

Our goal at the National Museum of Natural History/National Museum of Man is to excite your interest in the way the world works. We are sure that you will enjoy the things you will see here. We also hope you will learn things that can help us make the many decisions about our world that we will face in the coming years.

The Director

INTRODUCTION
TO THE MUSEUM

The National Museum of Natural History/National Museum of Man is dedicated to the collection, preservation, conservation, and selective exhibition of what is probably the largest assemblage of natural history specimens and human artifacts in the world. Its scientists and scholars conduct extensive original research on living and fossil animals and plants; rocks, minerals, and meteorites; and human origins, human biological diversity, and human cultures, ancient and modern. The Museum shares its work with the scholarly community through publications, symposia, and scholarly exchanges, and with the public through exhibitions, publications, and educational programs, in Washington, throughout the country, and internationally.

Each year some seven million people visit the Museum, which is the largest of the 16 museums of the Smithsonian Institution. Of the more than 134 million specimens and artifacts in the Smithsonian's legendary collections—ranging from aircraft and whale skulls to paintings and postage stamps—more than 118 million pertain to the natural sciences and belong to the National Museum of Natural History/National Museum of Man.

The act of Congress that established the Smithsonian Institution called for the collection, classification, and arrangement of "objects of natural history, plants and geological and mineralogical specimens." Thus, natural history collections have been a part of the Smithsonian from its beginnings in 1846. At the outset, the original Smithsonian Institution Building (the "Castle") housed the personal collections of James Smithson, the founder, and Spencer F. Baird, the second Secretary, in addition to collections gathered during early Smithsonian-sponsored field work and on several surveys organized under government auspices. These natural science collections grew enormously over the years, so in 1903, Congress appropriated funds for the Natural History Building, which opened in 1910. Since then, more than 125 million people have visited this building.

To accommodate large exhibitions, the museum building was originally planned as a great shell. Three-story-high halls, roofed with enormous skylights, radiated from the central four-story-high rotunda. A series of lower ceilinged exhibition halls flanked the major three-story-high axial halls. On the building's upper floors, laboratories, offices, and large attics were built—soon to be crammed from floor to ceiling with study collections. In 1961 and 1963, two wings for research offices and laboratories were added. In 1975, the West Court was built to provide more public space for a cafeteria, museum shop, Smithsonian Associates' dining room, and a new education facility, the Naturalist Center.

The National Museum of Natural History/National Museum of Man is the Smithsonian's most diversified as well as the largest science unit. Heir to the Institution's historically strong 19th- and early 20th-century efforts in biology, geology, and anthropology, the Museum today is the largest in the world in terms

Researchers stand in one of the many corridors in the Bird collection storage area, which holds a total of 450,000 bird skins.

Smithsonian naturalist Edward Nelson took this photograph of an Eskimo family in 1881—a rare document preserved in the Museum's National Anthropological Archives.

of the number of scientists engaged in museum-based natural history research. The growth and care of the collections, scholarly research, and dissemination of knowledge through publications, exhibitions, and educational programs remain the three cornerstones of the Museum's mission today.

The Collections

The National Museum of Natural History/National Museum of Man is responsible for encyclopedic collections of insects and other invertebrates; vertebrates such as fishes, amphibians, reptiles, birds, and mammals; plants; fossils; rocks, minerals, and meteorites; and anthropological artifacts. Most have been identified, classified, and cataloged, and they are stored "behind the scenes" in seemingly endless rows of storage cases, and in boxes, bottles, and vats on miles of racks and shelves.

A century and a half of field work in the natural sciences has yielded collections gathered from pole to pole and from every ocean and continent of the globe. These specimens, artifacts, field notes, and photographs form a major part of the known permanent record of modern and ancient life on Earth. They constitute a baseline for taxonomic (classification), ecological, paleontological, geological, evolutionary, developmental, and anthropological studies from which new knowledge is generated and against which it can be measured.

Each year more than three-quarters of a million specimens are added to this reservoir through gifts, purchases, expeditions of museum scientists, and deposits by government agencies. And each year more than 2,000 scholars visit the Museum to make use of the national collections, and more than 200,000 objects are loaned to the world's scientific community for research and exhibition elsewhere.

Old collections do not become antiquated or useless. On the contrary, their importance increases with time because they are frequently the only records that illustrate historical conditions now drastically changed or totally vanished. In some cases these collections include some of the Institution's rarest and most valuable national treasures.

To ensure the care, preservation, and accessibility of the collections, the Museum carries on a continual program of collection management, using computers to catalog and retrieve information, as well as to improve the quality of catalog data. In addition, the Museum is moving major portions of its collections to the Smithsonian's new Museum Support Center in nearby Suitland, Maryland—a state-of-the-art facility for collection storage, care, and study.

Research

The Museum's scientists are continually exploring the boundaries of knowledge in natural history; among their interests are the nature and history of the Earth and of its satellite, the Moon, and the larger universe; the history and diversity of life on Earth; and the development and variety of human populations and cultures. A major effort lies in systematic biology, concerned with the evolution, classification, and distribution of organisms and their relationships to their environments. Geologic studies of rocks,

A scientist digs for fossil fish in Fauquier County, Virginia.

minerals, ocean sediments, meteorites, and volcanoes are shedding light on the origin and history of the Earth and solar system. Work on fossil plants and animals documents and interprets the history of life on Earth and its relation to changing environmental factors such as climates and habitats.

Ongoing archaeological, ethnological, linguistic, and physical anthropological work includes studies of aboriginal cultures in the tropical forests and the Arctic; research on social and cultural history as well as contemporary life in various parts of the world; the search for humankind's earliest ancestors in Africa; evidence for the earliest colonization of the Western Hemisphere; and investigations of the skeletal biology of ancient and modern human populations. In addition, Museum anthropologists are producing *The Handbook of North American Indians*, a comprehensive, 20-volume encyclopedia designed for both scholarly and general readership.

Special consideration has always been given to the study of endangered cultures, species, and habitats, and their conservation. Ultimately, the Museum's basic research is reflected in advances in medicine, agriculture, exploration for minerals and other natural resources, and environmental protection. In 1987, a major program in the study and conservation of biological diversity was launched, with Smithsonian scientists taking a leading role in the urgent task of documenting the enormous diversity of life on Earth, especially in the tropical rain forests—ecosystems fast disappearing under the encroachment of rapidly increasing human exploitation.

In addition to their individual research programs, Museum scientists engage in interdisciplinary, cooperative research projects, both with colleagues here and in universities and museums around the world. Research annually leads to some 350 publications, which appear in book form or as articles in scientific journals or popular magazines.

The scientific program involves some 120 scientists and curators in seven research departments: Anthropology, Botany, Entomology, Invertebrate Zoology, Mineral Sciences, Paleobiology, and Vertebrate Zoology. Approximately 80 additional resident scientists from affiliated U.S. government agencies work closely with the Smithsonian staff. These agencies include the Department of Interior's Fish and Wildlife Service and U.S. Geological Survey, the Department of Agriculture's Systematic Entomology Laboratory, and the Department of Commerce's National Marine Fisheries Service Systematics Laboratory.

The Museum administers several other important scientific programs. The Smithsonian Oceanographic Sorting Center classifies animal and plant materials collected on oceanographic expeditions sponsored by the Smithsonian, other organizations, and federal agencies. These specimens are distributed for further study to an international network of researchers. The Scientific Event Alert Network notifies scientists worldwide of geophysical events such as volcanic eruptions and meteorite falls that might otherwise go unobserved scientifically. At the Smithsonian Institution Marine Station at Link Port, Florida, scientists are investigating the estuarine and marine environments along Florida's east coastline and adjacent oceanic waters, seeking basic information about the ecology and life histories of plants and animals living in subtropical waters and examining the chemical and physical features of these habitats.

A curator maps the forest canopy in Peru as part of the Museum's studies of biological diversity.

Sampling coral reefs off the coast of Belize helps scientists better understand these fascinating underwater structures.

The Museum Support Center

The new Museum Support Center at
Suitland, Maryland, provides ideal conditions for the storage and conservation
of collections, in addition to collection
study space. Most of its capacious storage area is devoted to the Museum's extensive holdings of scientific specimens
and human artifacts. A modern building
about six miles from the National Mall,
the Support Center provides storage in
four climate-controlled areas with collection storage equipment designed to
hold everything from the "wet" collections to meteorites and totem poles.

Exhibitions

The Museum's standing exhibitions feature many of the most spectacular and
informative objects from the collections
and focus on a diverse range of subjects:
the earliest traces of life; dinosaurs and
other fossil animals and plants; ice-age
mammals and the emergence of humans; origins of Western cultures; native
cultures of the Americas, the Pacific,
Asia, and Africa; minerals and gems;
geology of the Earth, Moon, and meteorites; bone structure; mammals and
birds of the world; insects and their relatives; and marine ecosystems, including
a living coral reef (the first exhibit of its
kind). Major renovations of many of
these exhibits are underway.

The Thomas M. Evans Gallery shows
important traveling exhibitions as well
as major special exhibitions organized
by the Museum. Small temporary exhibitions are regularly mounted in the Rotunda Gallery on the second floor. Book-

This corn portal marked the entrance to Seeds of Change, *the Museum's quincentennial commemorative exhibition. It was made of 14,000 ears of corn grown especially for the exhibit by farmers in New Mexico and Maryland.*

lets, summarizing the contents of some major, long-term exhibitions, are sold in the Museum Shop. Scholarly catalogs are often produced and sold for the Evans Gallery exhibitions.

Education

The Museum's Office of Education offers programs serving approximately 200,000 children and adults annually. Students from all over the United States visit the Museum for tours and other ac-tivities, an experience supplemented by a variety of booklets, teaching guides, and other educational materials produced and distributed by the office. A free film and lecture series is offered each Friday in the Baird Auditorium on the ground floor. Innovative educational facilities pioneered by the office include the Discovery Room, where persons of all ages may touch and examine natural objects, and the Naturalist Center, a resource and reference center, designed to

A living sculpture of a sauropod dinosaur greets visitors arriving at the Museum's Constitution Avenue entrance. Smithsonian horticulturists used three kinds of English ivy to create the topiary artwork.

provide a quiet atmosphere for study. A full range of public programming events accompanies each major exhibition in the Evans Gallery.

Museum scientists and curators are involved in many teaching activities, including classes sponsored by the Smithsonian's Resident and National Associates Programs, courses in nearby universities, and lectures to local schools and civic groups. They also direct the studies of a large number of young scholars and aspiring scientists who come to the Museum each year as interns and fellows.

A view of the eight-sided Rotunda, ringed with colorful banners marking some of the hall entrances.

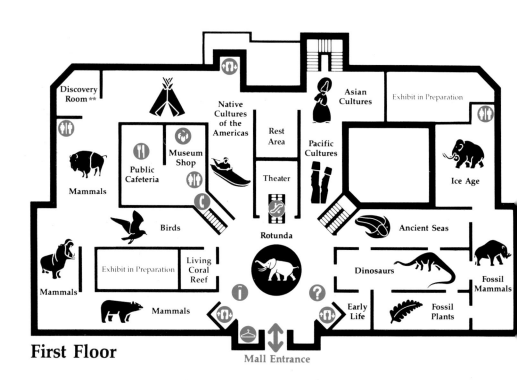

First Floor

THE EXHIBITIONS

FIRST FLOOR

THE ROTUNDA
Colorful banners ringing the Rotunda mark the entrances to some of the nearby exhibit halls. The Rotunda centerpiece and museum symbol is a giant bush elephant, a mounted specimen of the largest and most powerful land animal in the modern world.

FOSSILS: THE HISTORY OF LIFE
Exhibits in these halls recount the story of how, over more than 3.5 billion years, life in all its diversity evolved on the Earth. Myriad life forms have lived, undergone major transformations, and died on our constantly changing Earth. Fossils reveal important clues to this process, clues that enable scientists to reconstruct events in the distant past. But the fossils do not tell all, and there are plenty of unanswered questions—enough to keep paleontologists busy for a long, long time.

This exhibit area is divided into separate highlights, each one either marking an evolutionary milestone or explaining an aspect of the fossil record.

Earliest Traces of Life
A collection of rare vestiges of the very beginnings of Earth history are on view in this section. For example, the 3.8-billion-year-old rocks from western Greenland represent some of the oldest that scientists can ever hope to discover, because the Earth's natural processes probably have destroyed earlier ones. The round-edged pebbles and cobbles suggest that the Earth had cooled enough for running water to accumulate on its crust. Iron oxides indicate that free oxygen, while at very low levels, was present in the atmosphere.

Origins of Life
A timeline tracing the Earth's history from its birthday, about 4.6 billion years ago, to the present emphasizes that there is a tremendous expanse of time (85 percent) yielding only scant evidence of fossils, all of them microscopic organisms. Almost all the larger fossils found, such as those displayed in the neighboring halls, stem from the tiny, uppermost segment of the scale, which contains such forms of life as trilobites, dinosaurs, and humans.

The 4.6-billion-year-old Murchison meteorite, probably as old as the Earth itself, may yield clues to the birth of our solar system.

The 4.6-billion-year-old meteorite fragment that landed in Murchison, Australia, in 1969, is as old as the Earth itself, and is thought to be a remnant of the birth of the solar system. It contains amino acids, the building blocks of life.

Several exhibits nearby focus on questions of the origin of life on Earth. A light board demonstrates how most scientists think life arose from nonliving matter—through a series of intermediate chemical steps.

Enter Life, an animated film, presents possible scenarios for the origin of living things. The film explains one popular theory—that life began at the margins of warm little pools, where molecular chains could be periodically washed and dried.

The Earliest Ancestors

A dramatic mural depicts a hypothetical scene on Earth some 300 million years after the rocks from western Greenland were formed, 3.5 billion years ago. This scene, with its erupting volcano in the distance and its seemingly lifeless landscape, is an alien one. Nevertheless, early signs of life are present, namely, the mound-like masses jutting out of the sea.

These sediment accumulations, made by single-celled organisms, are called stromatolites. A 3.5-billion-year-old stromatolite forms the cornerstone of this hall, representing evidence of the oldest known ancestors of all forms of life, including humans.

Single-Celled to Multi-Celled Life

Exhibited are several primitive, single-celled organisms, mostly bacteria and

This dramatic mural depicts a hypothetical scene on the Earth, approximately 3.5 billion years ago, after the first living organisms had appeared.

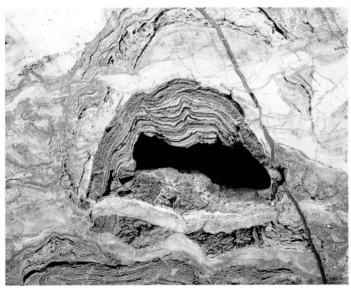

One of the oldest-known fossils—the earliest-known evidence of all forms of life—a 3.5-billion-year-old stromatolite.

The soft-bodied creatures modeled in this diorama are based on fossils that represent indisputable evidence of multi-celled life more than 570 million years ago.

blue-green "algae" (also bacteria), which lacked a nucleus (procaryotes). The emergence of organisms with nucleus-bearing cells (eucaryotes) represented a fundamental breakthrough, quickening the pace of evolution. The organized spirals and large size of the fossils from the Greyson Shale in Montana suggest that cells with nuclei and possibly multi-cellular life existed 1.3 billion years ago.

The Ediacaran fauna, first discovered in southern Australia, represents indis-putable evidence of multi-celled life. These are soft-bodied organisms, some of which resemble jellyfish and seg-mented worms, while others are unlike any living organisms yet found; they appeared about 570 million years ago. All lack the mineralized, rigid supporting skeletons and protective shells that characterize more advanced animals. Life in the Ediacaran Sea, a diorama, recreates an ocean aprowl with these bizarre organisms.

These fossil brachiopods and crinoids from the Life in the Ancient Seas *exhibit are more than 230 million years old. Descendants of these invertebrates, which ruled the sea during the Paleozoic era, are alive today.*

A display of fossils from the Mesozoic era (230–65 million years ago) shows how fish, marine reptiles, and ammonites were specialized for swimming and surviving in the sea.

During the Cenozoic era, which began about 65 million years ago, mammals that evolved on land invaded the sea. Fossils of ancient marine mammals, including a giant whale, are exhibited in front of a mural.

Life in the Ancient Seas

Life originated in the sea, and most fossils are the remains of sea creatures. This hall tells the story of sea life over time. Visitors entering are surrounded by the sound of waves, the effect of sunlight filtering through water, and overhead models of sea creatures. Two large murals illustrate fossil organisms as the living creatures they once were. The three exhibit sections chronicle the waxing and waning of life over three geological areas.

A walk-through recreation of a 250-million-year-old reef, with over 80,000 individual models, heralds the Paleozoic era. Trilobites, brachiopods, and crinoids epitomized this era. It ended with a devastating extinction that wiped out 80 percent of all sea life.

During the Mesozoic era bony fish and ammonites blossomed in diversity and abundance. Skeletons of sea turtles and ichthyosaurs provide evidence that some reptiles and birds evolved marine lifestyles during this time. A short ani-

A huge slab of an unknown animal's 505-million-year-old, chevron-shaped tracks, found in New York State.

mated film tells of the demise of many marine creatures at this era's close.

Mammals developed the ability to live in the sea during the Cenozoic era. Among the fossil skeletons on view are a 45-foot-long whale, dolphin, sea cow, and seal. Mollusks became very success-ful during this era. The final display pairs fossil clams and snails with their descendants living in modern seas.

The Paleozoic Era

At the beginning of the Paleozoic era, 570 million years ago, a dramatic explo-sion occurred in the preserved record of hard-shelled life. Compared to the mea-ger fossil finds of the Earth's early histo-ry, an astonishing increase now appears in the variety and number of fossilized animals. This is explained by the fact that animals with hard parts are much more likely than soft-bodied animals to have left traces in the fossil record.

The exhibit centerpiece is a huge slab of mysterious 505-million-year-old, chevron-shaped tracks, made by an un-known animal, which were discovered near Lake Champlain, New York. No known modern animal leaves a similar track pattern.

A diorama that reconstructs the soft-bodied marine fossils preserved in exquisite detail in the 530-million-year-old Burgess Shale of British Columbia. The Burgess Shale deposit was discovered in 1909 by the Smithsonian's fourth Secretary, geologist Charles D. Walcott.

In 1909, the Smithsonian's fourth Secretary, geologist Charles D. Walcott, discovered the 530-million-year-old Burgess Shale deposit in British Columbia. The remarkably preserved black-on-black fossils of this deposit yielded a surprisingly complete anatomical record of hard-bodied and many soft-bodied organisms. This find demonstrated the existence of diverse, complex soft-bodied creatures which must have had Precambrian ancestors that were never preserved. Some of these marine animals are so bizarre that all efforts to link them with any other known forms of life, past or present, have been unsuccessful.

By the end of the first 150 million years of the Paleozoic era (420 million years ago), most of the major invertebrate animal groups had produced the beginnings of rich and geographically widespread fossil records, including those of sponges, corals, starfish, and

One of the nearly 10,000 different species of trilobites—marine animals with jointed legs and segmented body coverings that were abundant at the very beginning of the Cambrian period (570 million years ago), but became extinct at the end of the Paleozoic era (240 million years ago).

many mollusks such as snails and clams.

A collection of trilobites, both large and small, is of particular note. These graceful and diverse marine animals, with their jointed legs and segmented body coverings, numbered close to 10,000 species before dying out at the end of the Paleozoic.

Two dioramas—one depicting life in a shallow sea that extended over most of Ohio, Kentucky, and Indiana during the

Delicate sea lilies such as these fossils were once abundant in the shallow seas that covered what are now parts of the Midwest.

Ordovician period, 440 million years ago, and another depicting life in a sea that covered most of eastern North America during the Silurian period, 420 million years ago—give flesh to this collection of marine creatures, many of which have surviving ancestors today.

Many of the echinoderms—a group of animals that includes starfish, brittlestars, sea urchins, sea cucumbers, sea lilies, and even the sand dollars you find out at the beach—are quite beautiful. Delicate fossil sea lilies, which lived 330 million years ago in seas that covered what is now Iowa and Indiana, are also beautifully preserved in a large slab of rock mounted on the wall.

Time and Fossils
Towering over this hall is a 27-foot-high time column. For humans with a life span of only about 80 years, geological time is nearly impossible to comprehend. This column serves as a time-orienting device, but represents less than one-sixth of total geologic history, 700 million years of the 4.6 billion years of the Earth, the time of the most abundant fossil remains.

The pageant of life is presented in a mural on the Time Column. This portion depicts the Age of the Reptiles, with the notorious Tyrannosaurus rex *at center.*

Five sides of the six-sided column convey time in different ways, but all correspond with one another. Thus, time is divided into the four geologic eras; 10-million-year increments; major evolutionary events; and the geologic periods. The fifth and most visually spectacular side of the column presents the pageant of life in a mural.

The floor-to-ceiling, 16-foot-tall fossil of **Callixylon**, *one of the earliest trees. Trees of this type grew 100 feet tall, 355 million years ago.*

Early Land-dwellers

Until the Silurian period, about 425 million years ago, life had existed only in the sea. Ultimately, however, the time came when some plants and animals pushed at the margins of their watery habitats and moved onto dry land.

A mural depicts the ancient world when its land surfaces were devoid of plants and animals, a short time before their migration from the seas began. A specimen of a tiny 400-million-year-old fossil plant from Wales, called *Cooksonia*, is evidence of one of the first pioneers. *Cooksonia* had an upright, self-supporting stem, a waterproof coating to protect it from the drying air, and a system of special cells to help in the transport of water into all parts of the stem.

Following *Cooksonia*, more and increasingly complicated plants appeared. Through fossils and graphics, the major plant groups of the Devonian period are introduced, as well as their water-dependent reproductive cycle, known as reproduction by spores. The exhibit also explains the evolution of the leaf, an invention that served to enlarge the surface area of a plant, thereby increasing the capacity for food manufacture through photosynthetic activity.

The First Trees

By the end of the Devonian period, about 360 million years ago, plants had developed the capacity for adding more layers of cells, both horizontally and vertically, to the internal structure of their stems. The additions increased the diameter of the stems, providing a firm foundation for growth, until the plants attained the size of trees. The huge, fossilized stump of the first known tree, *Eospermatopteris*, found in the first known forest, provides ample testimony to this innovation. A more dramatic visualization comes with the floor-to-ceiling, 16-foot-tall fossil of *Callixylon* (one of the other earliest trees). This specimen lived nearly 360 million years ago. Other specimens have been found that indicate trees such as this one could have been nearly 100 feet tall.

Amphibians

The evolution of the tree and the consequent establishment of the forests dramatically increased the food-producing capacity of the land. Thus the stage was set for the emergence of the first vertebrate animals to dominate the land—the amphibians. The first tetrapods to come out on land were probably the descendants of the lobe-finned fish.

On display is the fossilized crossopterygian-like skull and fishlike tail of one of the first known amphibians, *Ichthyostega*. Amphibians continued to evolve in a variety of shapes and sizes, including the pancake-flat *Buettneria* and the aquatic *Neopteroplax*. In the ensuing millions of years, other shapes appeared that resembled snakes and the familiar frog form that has remained the same for the last 180 million years.

The First Great Coal Period

From 345 to 280 million years ago, during the Carboniferous (Coal) period, amphibians and spore-bearing trees were the dominant animal and plant forms. During this interval, the Earth was covered with widespread, swampy, subtropical lowlands in which spore-bear-

The crossopterygians, a group of lobe-finned fishes of the Late Devonian period, had leglike, muscular fins, which they may have used to "walk" from drying stream beds downstream to larger pools of water. This kind of locomotion may have set the stage for the emergence of vertebrates on land.

ing trees, particularly the giant club-mosses and horsetails, thrived. After millions of years of burial and compression, the accumulated remains of this once lush vegetation were transformed into the great coal beds of Appalachia and other regions. On view are fossilized stumps, trunks, foliage, and spores from the great coal forests, including examples of scale trees, cordaites, calamites, and ferns.

In time, the world's climates became drier, coal forests became less prevalent, and spore-bearing plants were forced to give up their reign as the dominant plants of the Earth. Seed plants had been gradually evolving and were adapted for the new conditions. They were quick to achieve the prominence in the plant kingdom that they still hold today. At the same time, the amphibians were surpassed by the reptiles that evolved from them.

The Seed and the Egg
The parallel developments of the seed 350 million years ago and the egg 300

million years ago were tremendous breakthroughs for plants and animals. For the first time, reproduction was no longer tied to the water. A 70-million-year-old dinosaur egg from France symbolizes this liberation. The egg contained a protected, wet microhabitat for the developing reptilian embryo. The young reptile was ready for life in a land environment as soon as it hatched in a miniaturized adult form instead of having to pass through an aquatic larval stage as was and is the case with an amphibian.

Likewise, the earliest seed plants, the "gymnosperms" (Greek for "naked seeds"), provided a "care package" of food for their developing embryos within the seed. These plants shifted from dependence on water for the transfer of sex cells between individual plants to dependence on wind. The pollen grain, containing the male sex cells, is carried by the wind to the female reproductive organ, often a "cone," wherein the egg is subsequently fertilized. Today, the gymnosperms, which first appeared about

A 50-million-year-old fossil flower from shales of the Green River formation in Colorado.

A museum preparator works with the skeleton of **Eryops**, *an ancient amphibian. Its stout limbs and short body indicate that it spent much of its time on land.*

280 million years ago, include conifers, cycads, and ginkgos.

Flowering Plants

When flowering plants, the "angiosperms" ("covered seeds"), appeared about 105 million years ago, they added a bewildering variety of plants to the Earth. Today, virtually all the plants we eat and most of the plants we see are flowering plants. Flowering plants owe their success to three mechanisms: a more efficient water-conducting system, an energy-saving mode of reproduction, and a reliance on animals, most notably insects, for pollination. Insects accomplish this task inadvertently, while flying from flower to flower in search of food. Flowering plants can produce new generations with botanically unprecedented speed, certainly surpassing that of the gymnosperms.

A walk-through diorama recreates what is now the Washington, D.C., area, along the banks of the ancestral Potomac River, about 105 million years ago. Conifer forests flank the river, but the early flowering plants, looking like water and arrowhead lilies and shrubs, are also present. In the distance, a dinosaur adds a jarring touch to what would otherwise seem like a familiar scene.

A menacing but fantastic crowd of dinosaur reconstructions. The giant of the group is 80-foot-long Diplodocus longus.

Dinosaurs

"Life on land means walking, and walking means feet." Thus reads the caption beneath the elegant dinosaur foot marking the entryway to this highlight. The earliest known reptiles lived about 310 million years ago, and from the beginning two varieties are recognizable: stem reptiles and mammal-like reptiles.

The stem reptiles were small, insect-eating, lizard-like animals that gave rise to modern reptiles and birds, as well as dinosaurs. The earliest mammal-like reptiles were also lizard-like in appearance. They and their descendants dominated the terrestrial animal world for 125 million years before the dinosaurs arrived and eventually gave rise to mammals.

In the central gallery, dinosaurs, the great reptiles that inhabited the Earth for 140 million years, dominate the hall, as well as the entire multi-hall fossil complex. They are the best known of all fossil animals. A menacing but fantastic crowd of dinosaur reconstructions is congregated in the center of the gallery.

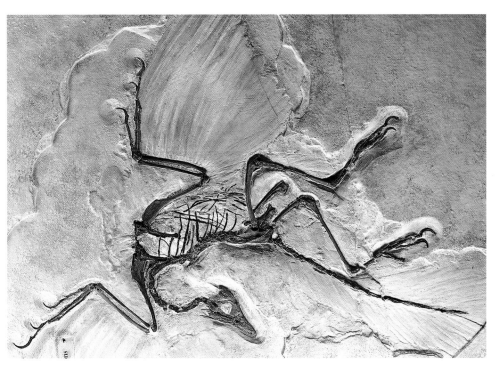

The feathers, toothy jaw, and clawed fingers preserved in this cast of Archaeopteryx—*the earliest known bird, demonstrate its descent from terrestrial reptiles.*

A life-size model of the plated, spike-tailed Stegosaurus.

Antrodemus, *a large meat-eating dinosaur, is portrayed in one of three mini-dioramas showing restorations of dinosaurs in their native habitats.*

On parade are the sharp-toothed, strong-jawed *Antromedus*, an aggressive predator capable of attacking other dinosaurs as large as the plated, spike-tailed *Stegosaurus*, which may be seen nearby in vintage 1904, papier-mâché model form. The giant of the group is the 80-foot-long *Diplodocus longus*, whose skeleton was found embedded in sandstone in Utah in 1923. It took one painstaking year to pry the fossil out of the rock and transport it to the Museum and another seven years to reconstruct its skeleton. Other dinosaurs in this group are the horned *Triceratops*, an adult and a juvenile *Camptosaurus*, and the notorious *Tyrannosaurus rex*, a dinosaur so terrifying that it gave a new definition to the word predator. Reaching 40 feet in length and 16 feet in height, *Tyrannosaurus rex* was the largest predator ever to walk the Earth.

The dinosaur reconstructions are peppered with displays that address common questions regarding these extraordinary animals. Were they hot or cold blooded? What and how did they eat? What were the circumstances of their discoveries? How are they reconstructed?

Of particular note are the casts of dinosaur eggs that were deposited 80 to 65 million years ago in what is now Montana by a small flesh-eater called *Troodon*. Lying there in a nestlike depression, these eggs remind us of the kinship of dinosaurs, birds, and all other reptiles. Despite the incredibly huge sizes of some dinosaurs, no eggs larger than a soccer ball are known. Scientists conclude from this that dinosaur young must have grown rapidly.

Anyone who has unsuccessfully attempted to put together a model ship or plane, with instructions, will understand the challenge facing the scientist who has to assemble a *Stegosaurus stenops* without instructions and with many missing parts. Field equipment, including sieves, picks, brushes, and other objects (that look as if they belong in a dentist's office rather than in a quarry) lie scattered around the dinosaur bones. These tools of the trade demonstrate that assembling a skeleton is only one part of a long process. First there must be a discovery, which sometimes is more by chance than by calculation. Then the easily shattered bones must be carefully extricated from the rock. To prevent breakage during excavation, the paleontologist sometimes uses a plaster jacket around the fossil-bearing rock, in the same way that a physician uses a cast to brace and correct broken bones in patients.

The Eleventh Hour, one of three minidioramas portraying the dinosaurs in their native environment, brings the dinosaur highlight of the exhibit to a close. Here, many of the dinosaurs whose fossil remains and reconstructions are on exhibit are seen amid the flowering plants that had become so much a part of the landscape, five million years before the dinosaurs became extinct, which was about 65 million years ago.

No one knows for sure why the dinosaurs vanished. Some scientists think that an asteroid or comet hit the Earth, creating an enormous dust cloud that blocked the sun, a disastrous ecological blow that caused mass extinction. Many paleontologists think that when global plate tectonics pushed the continents from one place to another, the cumulative small changes in climate and topography eventually became too much for these colossal reptiles to tolerate. Whatever caused the annihilation of the dinosaurs, their disappearance coincided with widespread extinction of many sea-dwelling invertebrates, plants, and reptiles. Any explanation for the disappearance of dinosaurs must also account for the extinction of these other groups, as well as for the survival of many kinds of marine organisms and, on land, mammals, birds, plants, and others.

Flight
This gallery display is the first of several highlights on the balconies overlooking the dinosaur gallery. It examines the evolutionary origins and special mechanisms of flight, a method of locomotion that has been in use for the past 300 million years. Using various fossil and modern-day examples, this exhibit underscores the difference between modern "true" flyers (bats, birds, and insects) and gliders (various snakes, frogs, squirrels, and fish), which simply "parachute" from one point to the next, often as a means of escape.

The main attraction—a life-size model of a pterosaur—is suspended from the ceiling. Called *Quetzalcoatlus northropi* after the Aztec god Quetzalcoatl, this long-necked flying reptile was twice as large as any bird that ever lived. It had a 36-foot wingspan and [we think] flew effortlessly on the thermal updrafts over what is now Texas and elsewhere. It is posed here in a gentle, banking dive, as

though in search of the meal it hasn't had in 65 million years.

Living Fossils
Many organisms have survived virtually unchanged for millions of years. Living specimens are displayed right next to fossils of their nearly identical ancestors. In this category are crocodiles, the burrowing brachiopod, and the gingko or maidenhair tree, with their ancestors dating back 100 million, 560 million, and 290 million years, respectively. Horseshoe crabs, common on sandy beaches, are survivors of arthropods that lived 550 million years ago, but they more closely resemble fossils from 150 million years ago.

Perhaps most intriguing is the model of a modern lobe-finned fish, the coelacanth. Until 1938, when one was discovered living off the coast of Madagascar, the coelacanth was thought to exist only in fossil form.

Fossil Ray-Fins
Fossil specimens show the evolution of this group of bony fishes that have populated the seas and fresh waters since the Devonian period, about 350 million years ago. Any fishing enthusiast could easily recognize many of the familiar species that sprang from this group, including sturgeons, catfish, carp, trout, and bass, as well as sea-dwellers such as tunas and swordfish.

Shark!
The razor-toothed jaw of the biggest shark that ever lived, *Carcharodon megalodon*, which became extinct only four

This life-size model of Quetzalcoatlus northropi, *with its 36-foot wingspan, is suspended over the dinosaur gallery.*

A Smithsonian model maker puts the finishing touches on a reconstruction of the razor-toothed jaws of the biggest white shark that ever lived— Carcharodon megalodon.

million years ago, is featured above the ramp. A 40-foot-long silhouette on the wall enables visitors to visualize its huge dimensions. It was more than twice as long as its close modern relative, the great white shark, whose jaw, teeth, and 16-foot-long silhouette, dwarfed by comparison, are also displayed.

Fossils as Natural Resources
The use of fossils in industry and everyday life is the subject of the final balcony highlight. Five 12-foot-high simulated outcrops of coal, phosphorite, limestone, diatomaceous earth, and petroleum are displayed along with details about their formation, extraction, and location of deposits throughout the world. Sample commercial products derived from these deposits are also shown.

Fossil Mammals
After the dinosaurs became extinct about 65 million years ago, mammals— furry, warm-blooded, mostly live-bearing animals—rapidly diversified and filled the empty niches.

At the entrance to the hall stands an 18-inch mammal skeleton in mid-leap over a piece of petrified wood. This fox-terrier-sized animal, named *Hyracotherium* but often called eohippus, is an ancestral horse. Its evolutionary story echoes throughout mammalian history. It was a forest-living leaf-eater, but its descendants adapted in stages to a climate that gradually became cooler, causing the forests to recede. Eventually, they evolved into modern horses.

The last 65 million years is called the Age of Mammals, but, in truth, this era

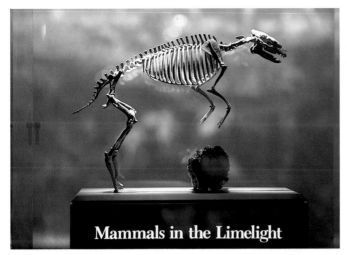

The skeleton of Hyracotherium, *an ancestral horse, marks the entrance to the fossil mammals hall.*

As visitors continue their walk through time, they pass early ancestors of modern dogs, pigs, rabbits, and squirrels.

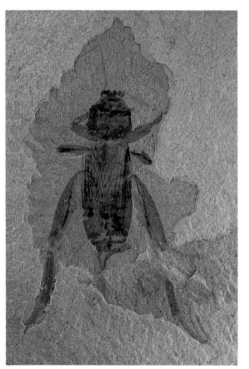

A 50-million-year-old fossil cricket preserved in shale of the Green River formation.

represents only one-third of mammalian history. A collection of tiny teeth and jaws of primitive mammals, ranging from 200 to 65 million years old, suggests that early mammals maintained a low profile as long as dinosaurs existed. Mammals remained small, nocturnal, and secretive, and were predominantly insect- and seed-eaters.

The Paleocene

The death of the dinosaurs left the land without large animals, a situation that mammals were quick to exploit during the Paleocene epoch (65–55 million years ago). During this 10-million-year time interval, mammals changed dramatically in size and diversity, with their average body mass increasing up to 10 times that of their predecessors. Some Paleocene mammals became large plant-eaters, while others became large flesh-eaters, preying upon their fellow mammals.

The Eocene

A rare glimpse into the warm, wet world of Eocene times (55–37 million years ago) is shown by fossil treasures of the Green River shales, deposits that accumulated on the bottom of a vast lake system that covered 5,000 square miles of what is now Utah, Colorado, and Wyoming.

Six huge murals depict life in the Eocene and subsequent epochs, two of which are a part of the Ice Age Mammals hall. Each provides a magnificent backdrop to fossils of mammals, birds, lizards, turtles, and plants of its time interval. Beside each specimen is a corre-

This is one of six murals depicting life from the Eocene epoch through the most recent Ice Age. Each mural provides a magnificent backdrop for fossil plant and animal assemblages from each time period.

sponding illustration, some reproduced from the murals, showing how the animal might have appeared in life. Many of these specimens were unearthed in the past century and a half in the American West by Smithsonian scientists. Included in the Eocene group is an important specimen, a nearly complete skeleton of *Smilodectes*, a lemurlike primate belonging to the order that includes humans.

Artists such as Jay Matternes and Bob Hynes, who painted these murals, base their work on careful anatomical study of the shape of joints and the position and strength of muscle attachments on fossil bones. This information, as well as paleoenvironmental studies, helps in recreating these early mammals and their habitats.

The Oligocene

Traveling from one time interval to the next, you will note that each has many of the same kinds of animals—horses, tapirs, rhinoceroses—but they change greatly from epoch to epoch. During the Oligocene period, from 37 to 23 million years ago, the first representatives of many modern families appear, including rabbits, dogs, pigs, beavers, and the oldest known member of the squirrel family.

A mural representing the extraordinary diversity of mammals that lived in the Miocene epoch (22.5 to 5 million years ago), when the climate cooled and grasslands spread dramatically.

The Miocene and Pliocene

During these epochs, from 23 to 3 million years ago, the climate continued to become cooler and the grasslands spread dramatically. Mammals adapted to the new environment. In a small theater, a mural, film, and specimens explain the evolution of horses, which, from the ancestral *Hyracotherium*, ultimately developed high-crowned, grass-processing teeth and the long legs that help an animal survive in open country.

ICE AGE MAMMALS

Ice Ages

The most recent two million years of the Earth's history, the Pleistocene, have been marked by cyclical cooling and warming of the climate. During the coldest glacial periods, vast sheets of ice spread over large portions of the northern continents. Vegetation patterns shifted and changes in animal distribution followed. Warmer intervals are called interglacial periods. A graph shows the

dramatic temperature changes in the Washington, D.C., area over the past one million years, suggesting that we are now in the midst of a warm period. Is this merely another interglacial period to be followed by another ice age?

A five-minute slide show provides a quick lesson on glaciation. The narrator reminds us that the temperate climate to which we have all grown accustomed is and has been subject to change. The evidence of past climates is all around us. Spectators leave the theater with enough visual clues to recognize some common glacial features when visiting areas once affected by glacial activity.

Land Bridges

During the Ice Age, an enormous quantity of water was locked up in land ice, causing the sea level to drop and expose land connections between continents and islands that were previously isolated. Consequently, many animals previously native to one continent spread to other areas. In addition, geologic forces sometimes created new connections, as

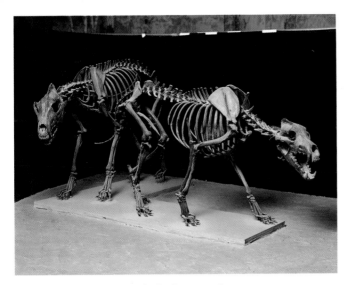

The sticky pools of the Rancho La Brea tar pits, now surrounded by downtown Los Angeles, led many Pleistocene (Ice Age) mammals to their death, including these dire wolves.

was the case with the Central American Land Bridge, which allowed a number of South American animals to migrate into North America, and vice versa.

Pleistocene Preservation

Most of the fossilized land mammals seen up to this point were found in flood-plain deposits. In the Ice Age, other methods of fossilization were of special importance. On view are the bones of animals that were unwittingly mired in the sticky pools of the Rancho La Brea tar pits, now surrounded by downtown Los Angeles. The two most common animals excavated from that site are the dire wolf and the saber-toothed cat, predators that were apparently lured to the pit by the promise of easy prey and then became stuck themselves.

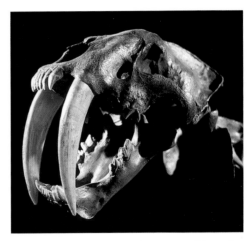

A saber-toothed cat skull, also recovered from the Rancho La Brea tar pits, bares its stabbing canine teeth.

Another source of Pleistocene fossils spotlighted in this hall is permafrost. In areas of permanently frozen ground, animals such as the mummified bison and horse on display fell into pits made by meltwater in the frozen subsoil and were killed. Their carcasses were quickly frozen and remain intact to this day.

Mammoths and Mastodons

The woolly mammoth, and its somewhat smaller relative, the mastodon, are the two animals that probably best symbolize the latest Ice Age. Mammoths, with their thick, shaggy coats and high-crowned, rasplike teeth, were adapted to life in harsh, cold climates and munched on the coarse, tough grasses of northern Eurasia and North America. Mastodons had teeth with rounded cusps and browsed on the leaves and twigs of the vegetation in the warmer woodland areas of North and South America. The curious skeletons of mammoths and mastodons were the first fossils to receive truly scientific attention in the 19th century, and these studies formed the roots of the science of vertebrate paleontology.

Gigantism

The succession of climatic changes that produced shifts in land areas and environments during the Pleistocene probably also resulted in the phenomenon of gigantism. Some of the largest known species of birds and mammals developed during this period, evolving in areas isolated by geographic or environmental barriers. For example, the now extinct moa of New Zealand, in the absence of mammalian predators, became

The woolly mammoth—an extinct elephant species that once abounded in North America and northern Eurasia—reached gigantic size during the latest Ice Age.

very large and gradually lost its capability to fly.

Gigantic size ultimately proved to be a disadvantage in the Pleistocene's quickly changing environments. For instance, the Irish elk were victims of their amazingly large antlers, which proved to be a hindrance when their grassy range was replaced by forests.

The Emergence of Man

Early in the Pleistocene, hominids were restricted by limited cultural and technological achievements to tropical and subtropical environments. However, the development of unique cultural adaptations such as stone tools, fire, and hunting allowed the human species to expand into new regions and lifestyles and ultimately to dominate other animals and environments.

The giant deer's amazingly large antlers proved to be a hindrance when its grassy range was replaced by forests.

Early belief in a spiritual world is suggested by this reconstruction of a Neanderthal cave burial thought to have taken place about 70,000 years ago.

Six skulls illustrate the physical development of humans from a shorter, smaller-brained ancestor to a taller, bigger-brained modern form (*Homo sapiens sapiens*), which emerged at least 35,000 years ago. The skulls are supplemented by reconstructions of important Pleistocene archeological sites and associated tool industries. Sites and artifacts are displayed in a steplike fashion, emphasizing how human advancement has been marked by lessening physical differences and increasing cultural diversity.

A fired clay animal figurine and a woman carved from mammoth ivory, both from the Upper Paleolithic, are among man's early attempts at artistic expression. Early ancestral belief in a spiritual world is poignantly displayed in the reconstruction of a Neanderthal cave burial that took place in southern France, 70,000 years ago, a dramatic conclusion to this major exhibit.

This carved wooden figure comes from the Ivory Coast.

This "Head of Queen Mother" is a sample of bronze casting from the old Benin Kingdom of southwestern Nigeria, where this art had great religious significance.

AFRICAN, ASIAN AND PACIFIC CULTURES

Africa

Africa's most striking characteristics are its immense size and wide diversity of peoples, cultures, and languages. More than three times the size of the continental United States, Africa today represents a complicated conglomeration of over three hundred million people, inhabiting more than 50 countries. The African continent is not only divided by the boundaries of its nation-states, but also is composed of diverse language groups, cultures, ecological zones, and histories. An all-new exhibit currently under development will highlight this diversity and its impact on the Americas.

Asia

Common throughout Japan are Shinto shrines similar to one shown as a model in a small diorama. Both Buddhism and the ancient Shinto religion play an important part in Japanese daily life and thought.

In the middle of the 17th century, Japan, fearful of an onslaught of foreign influences, firmly shut her gates for 250 years against traders and explorers. Under military rule, the society was divided into four strata, including the samurai, who made up about 8 percent of the population and were highest on the social ladder. They enjoyed many privileges and lived by an exacting code of honor. Several of Japan's most eminent armorers made components of the samurai suit on display here.

The Chinese have traditionally enjoyed a highly developed theatrical tradition; many thousands of stage performances are given each day all over

In this scene from a traditional Chinese opera, advisers warn the queen mother of a plot to usurp the throne of the infant emperor of the Ming dynasty.

China for visitors and factory workers and in schools and public halls. A scene from one such performance is depicted in a diorama. In this exhibit (accompanied by a musical recording), a company dramatizes the salvation of an important Ming dynasty family from an evil regent's plot to unseat the infant heir. One moral is: good cannot come from evil. While modern China has discarded such stories, this musical medium is still used to convey moral themes.

The Chinese written language is shared by literate speakers of all China's many languages and dialects. This system is made up of tens of thousands of symbols or characters, many of which first originated as "pictographs," or stylized depictions of common objects. Various styles of this calligraphy are on view. Writing brushes, ink stones and sticks, and water droppers are all components of the calligrapher's toolkit.

At the intersection of the Asian and Pacific halls stands the brightly dressed Kathakali dancer, portraying a wicked king in a South Indian Hindu epic. This type of dancing involves years of training and elaborate costuming. Eye movements and hand gestures are important features of this form of dance. Exhibits ringing the Kathakali dancer focus on the toys, jewelry, religious architecture, and arms and armor of India and Pakistan.

The Pacific
To best understand this hall, begin at the Rotunda entrance where a large map with carved figures beneath it introduces the five major areas of the Pacific. The artifacts and works of art in this hall reflect the diverse cultural, environmental, and historical backgrounds of people who live in Polynesia, Micronesia, Melanesia, Australia, and Indonesia. Many of these specimens are among the oldest objects in the Museum. They were collected on an exploring expedition led by Charles Wilkes between 1838 and 1842. Today, life in the Pacific is considerably different. Nonetheless, these

This dancer portrays a wicked king in a South Indian Hindu epic.

Members of the Maori tribe of New Zealand tattoo a fellow Maori.

A stone statue carved of soft volcanic rock from Easter Island in the South Pacific.

One of the largest "coins" ever used—a stone disk from the Micronesian island of Yap.

objects from the past will help visitors better understand the diversity and traditions of the present-day peoples of the Pacific.

Polynesia Like other Polynesians, Easter Islanders had a large variety of sacred places used for burials and religious ceremonies. Stone busts carved of soft volcanic tuff, sometimes as tall as 33 feet and weighing as much as 90 tons, were often erected at these sites. These monuments probably commemorated illustrious ancestors who brought benefit to their living descendants.

The scene depicted in a nearby diorama shows the interrelationship of art and social organization. Members of the Maori tribe of New Zealand, the largest land area in Polynesia, are using a chisel-like implement and soot to tattoo a fellow Maori. The tattoo indicated rank and authority throughout Polynesia.

Polynesians were born into a social class and were bound together in a web of kinship and social obligations. Chiefs formed an aristocracy and were given status, prestige, and certain personal privileges in accordance with their social rank. Fans, flywhisks, staffs, stools, and kava-drinking were all symbols of rank and prestige.

49

Chiefly prerogatives included access to the most beautiful and valued items of clothing and ornament. Most clothing was fashioned from the beaten inner bark of the paper mulberry plant, but the most elegant of all Polynesian apparel were Hawaiian capes made of tiny red and yellow feathers. They were worn only by the highest members of ancient Hawaiian society, such as male chiefs and kings. The cloak-making process was long and delicate. It is estimated that 450,000 feathers were used in long cloaks.

Micronesia The 2,500 islands of Micronesia are scattered over an area larger than the United States, but consist of only 1,260 square miles of land. As island-dwellers, Micronesians are intimately linked to the sea, and their survival depends on knowledge of it. All Micronesian cultures are concerned with three important aspects of the sea—how to get across it, how to exploit it for food, and what to do when devastation strikes.

Micronesians navigated by the apparent motion of the sun and stars, the direction of the wind, the ocean currents, the wave patterns on the surface of the sea, and the flight of birds. In the Marshall Islands, stick charts, similar to maps, were used for teaching navigation. Cowrie shells were used to fix positions between atolls and curved sticks were used to illustrate different wave patterns. Another specialty of Micronesians was very fine weaving done on horizontal looms.

On display is one of the largest "coins" ever used, the calcite stone disk from the Micronesian island of Yap. It is six inches thick and seven feet in diameter. In pre-European days, Yap islanders sailed nearly 300 miles to the Palau Islands to quarry these disks, carrying them back in specially built canoes. The ownership of the coin might change, but often its location did not.

Melanesia In Melanesia and New Guinea, the functional political unit was often only a single village. The headsman often achieved his position by ability and personality and acquired status by creating a following. Elaborate rituals and dramatic ceremonies were presented and were occasions for spectacular displays of the visual and performing arts.

Representative works of art, shown in two cases, illustrate the artistic emphasis on the human body and especially the head. The material from Fiji demonstrates its transitional status between Polynesia and Melanesia. Bark cloth and whales' teeth were the most valued objects to Fijians and were used primarily by chiefs.

Australia The Aborigines of Australia based their subsistence primarily on hunting and gathering and were renowned as adept hunters. A skillful spearthrower could judge the distance that a kangaroo covers between hops and aim the spear in front of the animal before its next spring. The best known Aboriginal weapon is the boomerang, which could be used to hunt kangaroos or as a fighting weapon. A good fighter could, with a flick of his wrist, make a boomerang go straight to an opponent or fly at him on a curved course.

Above: The Discovery Room welcomes visitors of all ages to see and touch many natural history objects.

Bottom Photo: *Visitors explore the contents of several discovery boxes made available in the Discovery Room. They can select from more than 30 boxes, each focusing on a different topic.*

In contrast to their simple hunting and gathering technology, Aborigine life is a maze of strict taboos, social customs, and relationships, making their social structure among the most complex in the world. The northern Aborigines of Arnhem Land were famous for their bark paintings, which represent mythical beings and events. Because these paintings were associated with male activities, women and uninitiated boys were forbidden from seeing them on penalty of death.

DISCOVERY ROOM

Wandering through this museum, you may often feel tempted to touch its manifold and curious objects. The Discovery Room, while primarily geared toward young children, allows visitors of all ages to handle unusual natural history and anthropological specimens.

Some objects, housed on open shelves or in special containers, are accompanied by tags that identify them or ask puzzling questions to arouse curiosity. Here, children may touch a snake skin, count the rattles on a rattlesnake, compare the smooth, rounded cusps of a mastodon tooth with the rough, flat ridges of a nearby mammoth tooth, discover the magnetic qualities of a lodestone, or try on clothing from other countries and then look at themselves in a nearby mirror. Also on view is the boniest Smithsonian resident, "Boney Toney," a completely articulated human skeleton wearing a staff identification badge. Discovery boxes encourage you to touch, examine closely, and use all your senses in the same way a scientist does.

A little humor is enjoyed in this diorama depicting a traditional family of Polar Eskimos of Smith Sound, Greenland.

This 19th-century Arapaho tipi, constructed with 14 buffalo hides, was among the Smithsonian exhibits displayed at the Philadelphia Exposition of 1876.

NATIVE CULTURES OF THE AMERICAS

Totem poles, birch bark canoes, feather headdresses, and painted pottery have become stereotypical trademarks of the American Indian. You may be surprised to discover that this picture is a composite one, formed of bits and pieces from distinct geographic regions and Indian cultures. These cultures have undergone radical changes since the arrival of Europeans, particularly in the 20th century. This hall, constructed in the 1950s, represents these cultures as they were before rapid acculturation took place in the 20th and late 19th centuries.

From the Rotunda, you will start in Greenland and travel south to Tierra del Fuego at the tip of South America. You can learn about the many ways Indian tribes in North and South America exploited their natural resources for food, clothing, and shelter, as well as learn about transportation, warfare, religion, and everyday implements. Some of these artifacts were collected by early explorers; others were collected later under the auspices of the fledgling Smithsonian Institution by correspondents, explorers, and Army Medical Corps officers who served at military posts on the western frontier during the 19th century. The hall is organized geographically according to the culture area concept, which is based on the idea that cultural differences among Native Americans developed in response to varying ecological conditions.

Polar Eskimos

At the entrance to this hall is a life-size group depicting a family of Polar Eskimos of Smith Sound, Greenland. In the foreground, a young boy is bent over a very small seal that he has clubbed. Beyond him stand members of his family, including his father who is laughing because his son has called for the dog team to bring home such a little animal.

Woodland Indians

Indian tribes from this region faced a very different set of environmental challenges from the Eskimo. The Chippewa birch bark canoe, the traditional vehicle of people of the northern woodlands, was used in hunting, fishing, gathering wild rice, and transportation.

The frightening masks nearby were created in part by members of a curing society called the Iroquois False Face Society. They first carved features representing spiritual beings on a living tree, then cut the mask free. The masks were worn during curing rituals held for sick members of the society.

Plains Indians

Plains Indian life revolved around the American bison, or buffalo, which was used for food, clothing, shelter, and in many other ways—some examples of which are on display.

Hides of 14 buffalo were laced together to construct the Arapaho tipi in the center of this hall. This tipi was among the Smithsonian exhibits displayed at the Philadelphia Centennial Exposition of 1876.

Until 1880, only the Plains Indians wore colorful feather bonnets like the one on view. However, the feather headdress eventually became a universal symbol of the American Indian.

Most visitors are familiar with the Sioux chief, Sitting Bull, whose Winchester, on display here, was donated by the family of the officer to whom Sitting Bull surrendered. The 13-shot, repeating rifle was probably superior to those guns used by the soldiers at the Battle of Little Big Horn, in which General Custer's cavalrymen were defeated by Indians under Sitting Bull's command. Also displayed in this collection is a Blackfeet two-edged stabber, collected during 1853 overland expeditions by those mapping railroad routes, and a stone-headed war club collected by Lewis and Clark during the first decade of the 19th century.

Pacific Northwest Coast Indians

A major concern in the lives of many Northwest Coast tribes has been the relative social status of the groups to which they belong. Such status is established and maintained through the accumulation and distribution of food, blankets, works of art, and other valued goods. Individuals belonging to the Kwakiutl or neighboring tribes attempted to validate or improve their community status by holding "potlatches," occasions where the host tried to outdo his rivals by showering his guests with gifts and even destroying valuable things to indicate indifference to property.

Art, particularly beautiful carving, in relief or in the round, was highly developed on the northwestern Pacific coast. It was an extension of Northwest Coast Indian society, often depicting group or individually owned symbols or crests. To render these symbols recognizable, certain distinctive features were selected and consistently used, making the general style highly standardized. The exhibit includes a newly installed case of masks from various tribes of the Northwest Coast. A nearby film, which incorporates old and new film of a Kwakiutl potlatch, shows what these masks might have looked like in use.

Totem poles also bore these telltale crests, but were erected for many different reasons. There were memorial poles raised by a deceased chief's heir as part of the succession process and mortuary poles erected alongside a deceased chief's grave. These totem poles advertised special privileges and consisted of symbols or crests representing important events in family history, including legendary encounters with spirits and monsters.

More Cultures

Additional displays offer a sampling of the cultural specialties developed by Indian tribes from northern California to South America. Life-size dioramas interspersed among other exhibits permit visitors to watch the Hupa Indians processing acorns, study Pueblo pottery-making, visit a Hopi apartment, or witness a Hopi Snake Dance.

You can admire the beautifully embroidered Mexican Huichol sash, pouch, cape, and shirt displayed on a life-size figure. Brightly painted and comical modern Mexican papier-mâché figures are part of a traditional celebration of All Soul's Day.

From the Caribbean, a mini-diorama turns the tables on history by presenting the 1492 discovery of Columbus by the Lucayan Indians of the Bahamas. The

Art, particularly beautiful carving in relief, was highly developed by tribes of the Northwest Coast. This conventional animal design was carved on the side of a box made by a member of the Haida tribe.

Zuni pottery pieces reflect a traditional art that is still alive today.

This Antarctic diorama contains specimens collected by one of Admiral Richard E. Byrd's parties. The largest of penguins, the emperor penguin, and the small Adelie penguin are featured here.

accent is on Lucayan culture, and a case beside the diorama contains a skull, pots, beads, charms, and other materials collected on a 1947 Smithsonian expedition to what was believed by some to be the original site of Columbus's landing.

Exhibits on the southernmost American Indians living near Tierra del Fuego in South America conclude this hall.

BIRDS

Birdwatchers may leave their binoculars behind when they enter this hall. A veritable worldwide aviary, it allows the serious student to study aspects of bird evolution, distribution, ecology, and classification and the casual visitor simply to enjoy the beauty and diversity of birds.

You will see birds from the major geographic regions of the world, in dioramas of natural settings and in special topical cases. The diversity of birds is shown by representatives of all 27 orders—a sample of the 8,700 known species of birds.

Many bird species are colonial nesters. Some, like the palm chat of the West Indies, build their nests so closely together that they combine to form a large apartment house. Each nest, however, remains independent of the others and has its own entrance.

One group—the birds of paradise—received its name from seafarers of old who were convinced the birds were wanderers from a celestial paradise. The males have spectacular plumage and are also noted for their strange and beautiful dance movements, both of which they display in courtship. The blue bird of paradise, with a trapeze artist's ease, displays its bright blue plumes while hanging upside down, and the Wallace's standard wing performs a backward somersault from its perch.

After viewing what many consider the most beautiful of all birds, you will find a diorama displaying one of the most bizarre—bower birds, a family restricted to Australia and New Guinea. Unlike the closely related birds of paradise, these birds lack highly ornamental plumes, but the males compensate for this by constructing and sometimes decorating bowers or display grounds to attract females.

The satin bower bird paints the walls of its bower with a mixture of saliva and chewed up fruits, grass, rotten wood or charcoal. To apply the "paint," it manufactures wads of fibrous bark to use as paint brushes, representing one of the rare instances of tool-making by an animal.

Protection of the young is a primary concern of most birds. The rhinoceros hornbill nests in holes high up in the tall trees of the Malay Peninsula, Sumatra, and Borneo. When the female is about to lay her eggs, she—from inside the nest—and her mate—from outside—plaster up all but a small part of the entrance with mud, dung, and other materials. The male feeds the female through this tiny opening until the young are ready to fly. In the meantime, the developing young nestle within their fortress, safe from snakes, monkeys, and other enemies. The female and young eventually dig their way out of the nest.

In the reconstructed snow-dotted environment of an area below Mount Vernon, Virginia, it may amaze you to spot the exotic, green, yellow, and orange hues of the Carolina parakeet. The only species of parrot ever native to the eastern United States, this bird is now extinct.

Another bird now among the ranks of the extinct is the passenger pigeon—one of the most gregarious of birds. Single flocks were estimated to number over a billion individuals, forming clouds overhead. Excessive hunting and the massive loss of forests cleared for agriculture brought about the extinction of this species. On display nearby is Martha, the last individual of this species, who died on September 1, 1914, in the Cincinnati, Ohio, zoo.

Sometimes birds and other animals develop peculiar food-getting relationships. The greater honey guide feeds on beeswax and, sometimes, larvae and eggs in bee hives. However, it cannot always gain access to hives hidden in hollow trees or termite nests by itself. The honey guide solves this problem by leading animal accomplices to the hives, which do the heavy work of tearing them open. They help themselves to the contents and leave the remainder for the bird. The honey guide will enlist the aid of the ratel, a large African weasel exhibited here, baboons, and even humans, leading them on treasure hunts

A male rhinoceros hornbill feeds its mate through a tiny opening in their fortresslike nest, designed to keep her and her developing young safe from enemies.

that can last from a few seconds to an hour.

The largest of all living birds, the ostrich, is also highlighted in a diorama. Ostriches lay their eggs in walled nests—which usually measure almost 10 feet in diameter—on dry, sandy river beds and other sandy spots. Before hatching, social contact between the ostrich chicks and the parents, as well as among the chicks, is established by their peeps. In the still unpipped eggs, the chicks utter various social calls, which trigger pecking at the shell and prepare parents for the appearance of their offspring.

MARINE ECOSYSTEMS
Normally, only a handful of scientists ever have the opportunity to study the ocean's depths, but in this hall the ocean, with its teeming life, washes up to museum visitors each day.

Two 3,000-gallon aquarium systems contain two fascinating ocean environments—the subarctic waters of the Maine coast and the warm, tropical coral reefs of the Caribbean. Residents of the murkier cold-water tank include kelp, rockweed, marsh grass, lobsters, scallops, mussels, hake, tomcod, and scaup. Colorful inhabitants of the coral reef tank include blue-green, green, and red algae; living corals; sea anemones; tube worms; surgeon fish; parrot fish, squirrel fish, and crabs.

Do not be alarmed if you spy an occasional mermaid or merman behind the coral reef tanks. These figures are simply the scientists in the adjacent laboratory who are studying these ocean communities. In addition, like the Wizard of Oz in his booth, they orchestrate the electronic, mechanical, and biological devices that mimic the tides and the changing seasons, as well as recreate night and day.

Hanging in the middle of this cavernous hall is the largest single exhibit in the Museum, the life-size, 92-foot model of a blue whale—the biggest animal that has ever lived, and now a highly endangered species. Instead of teeth, the blue whale possesses a series of horny palatal plates fringed with coarse bristles called baleen. It feeds by taking in large quantities of water containing small organisms such as sardines, shrimplike krill, and plankton. It then closes its mouth and forces water through the sieve of baleen plates, trapping thousands, sometimes millions of these organisms and then dislodging them from the baleen with its tongue.

Martha, the last individual of her species—the passenger pigeon—died on September 1, 1914, in the Cincinnati, Ohio, zoo.

An ostrich—the largest of all living birds—is displayed with chicks and some unhatched eggs.

The life-size, 92-foot-long model of a blue whale—the largest animal that has ever lived.

The renovation of this hall, currently underway, will highlight the diversity of organisms found in the marine environment. On display will be fish, mammals, sea stars, shells, and a rare giant squid—a sea animal that for centuries has stimulated imaginations and given rise to fantastic tales and myth. Only the third giant squid ever recovered on the United States coast, it is preserved as it was found after being washed ashore in February 1980 on Plum Island, north of Boston, Massachusetts.

At the foot of the hall stands an imposing mounted specimen of the largest of the fin-footed aquatic mammals—the walrus. Its tusks serve many functions, ranging from ice-choppers to head props to defense. Sometimes the tusks even function as a fifth limb when the

Living models of two marine ecosystems, the Maine rocky coast and Caribbean coral reef, demonstrate what ecosystems are and how they work.

In the coral reef model, a yellow tang searches for food while clownfish hover in the protective tentacles of soft corals.

A herd of African hartebeest, accompanied by a single straight-horned oryx, greets visitors to the Mammals hall.

walrus emerges from water and climbs onto the ice. Visitors may conclude their visit to this hall by watching a delightful film about pinnipeds—a group of mammals that includes seals and the sea lion, in addition to the walrus.

MAMMALS

A herd of African hartebeest with their sandy-colored coats stands at the entrance to this hall. All living mammals have backbones, feed their infants milk, have only a single bone on each side of the lower jaw, and three sound-transmitting bones in the inner ear. But despite these shared features, the essential fascination of mammals lies in their diversi-

ty—of form, function, and, above all, individual behavior. The hartebeest standing on the anthill in this diorama, for instance, is serving as a sentinel, watching for danger.

There are three major types of living mammals—placental, marsupial, and monotreme—comprising 18 orders and about 4,000 species. Half of these species are rodents and a quarter are bats. An exhibit with models of bat heads demonstrates the wide variety of facial characteristics within this large group. They range from elfin to doglike to the grotesque. Most of the variation is related to specialized food-gathering activities or navigation with ultrasounds.

Some mammals undergo remarkable

The cats—one of several mammal families that are grouped together for display.

CATS OF THE WORLD

Mounted specimens of the primate order, a group that includes humans and encompasses a wide array of mammals occupying an extensive range of habitats.

population fluctuations, as seen on the chart of lemming mass migrations in Norway between 1862 and 1939. In Norway, these short-tailed, chunky rodents live on mountaintop heaths, where their population periodically becomes very dense. To escape the pressure, they gradually move in the only direction they can—downhill. At lower elevations they find no suitable habitat, and eventually most of the migrants die of starvation, predation, or drowning in lakes, rivers, or even the sea. The migrations may be a result of several causes: depletion of food supplies and shelter or overcrowding.

Mammal family groups displayed throughout the hall include: the cats, most of which are bedecked with black circles, stripes, rosettes, spots, and other patterns; the bears, the world's largest terrestrial carnivores; the wild pigs and boars, with their coarse, bristly coats and tusks; and the dogs, ranging in size from the tiny fennec to the large Arctic wolf.

Variation within an order is shown for the primates, a group that includes humans. This lineage encompasses a wide array of mammals occupying an extensive range of habitats. Mounted specimens of lemurs, lorises, tarsiers, monkeys, and a gorilla are all on view. In cases above eye level, agile gibbons swing, orangutans hang, and a proboscis monkey relaxes.

The cat-sized Virginia opossum—the only marsupial native to the United States—is spotlighted in a woodland diorama. Marsupials, a group that includes kangaroos, give birth to young at an early stage in their development. They complete their growth attached to nipples in the mother's pouch.

Climate leaves its stamp on animal adaptation. For instance, jerboas—small, desert-dwelling rodents—have elongated hind limbs and other adaptations for jumping, their primary mode of locomotion. In an arid environment, jumping conserves energy by getting an animal farther faster. It is also a valuable defense strategy, particularly when combined with the jerboa's ability to "ricochet" and thereby confuse predators.

The red wolf, a placental mammal, and the Tasmanian wolf, a marsupial, once roamed the southeastern United States and Australia, respectively. Though unrelated, they both adapted in similar ways to similar environments in different parts of the world. Both are now extinct (or close to it).

The quills or spines that protect animals like the hedgehog, porcupine, and echidna provide examples of similar adaptations developing independently among unrelated animals, a principle called convergence.

Some mammals have developed the amazing ability to navigate using their sense of hearing. By producing ultrasonic sounds (sounds above the limit of human hearing), which are reflected back to them as echoes, these mammals can locate specific objects, such as obstacles and prey. Most bats, whales, porpoises, and some shrews have this capacity. The sonar of submarines is based on the same principle of echolocation. In the case of bats, their elaborate "leafy" noses may act to modify, direct, and focus these ultrasonic sounds, allowing them to pinpoint insects, flowers, and other prey, and determine the ripeness of fruit.

The coats of mammals often appear to be color-coordinated with the surrounding environment, which helps conceal them from predators. Desert rodents of New Mexico offer a prime example of this camouflage phenomenon. In adjoining areas, white sands are inhabited by populations of nearly white individuals, while in stretches of black lava live populations of blackish individuals of the same species. Likewise, many northern mammals have white winter coats that are replaced in springtime by darker summer coats. Camouflage is often a means of survival among animals. You will see it again in the Insect Zoo.

Many of the African mammal specimens in the rest of this hall were collected by President Theodore Roosevelt during his 1909–10 African expedition, sponsored by the Smithsonian Institution. Today, if you were to go on a picture-taking safari, you probably would still see these same animals in the wild. Here in the hall you will see Thompson's gazelle, with its conspicuous black side-bands; the square-lipped rhinoceros, with its two horns and a tick bird on its back; Grevy's zebra, with its dizzyingly narrow black and white stripes; a hippopotamus caught in a yawn; a male lion with its pride; and the African buffalo, distinguished by its Viking helmet-like horns, which are effective anti-predator devices.

Certain mammals, such as flying lemurs and flying squirrels, are accomplished aerial acrobats. Flying lemurs or colugos have a gliding membrane that stretches from the side of the neck to the tips of the fingers and toes, continuing to the very tip of the tail. No other gliding mammal has such an extensive membrane. Flying lemurs can execute controlled glides of 230 feet or more. By comparison, flying squirrels have a membrane that stretches only between limbs, and a free tail that serves as a rudder.

NORTH AMERICAN MAMMALS

You don't have to leave American soil to find spectacular mammals, as demonstrated by the American species highlighted in this hall. Visitors viewing these beautifully crafted dioramas can almost feel the chill of Mount McKinley (now Denali) National Park after a snowfall, the unsteady footing of a shale ledge in the Canadian Rockies, or a breeze sweeping along the grasslands of western North Dakota—just three of the scenic spots chosen as appropriate backdrops for mammals in this exhibit hall.

Moving through the hall, you will see the Alaskan caribou with antlers looking like flat palms with protruding fingers; giant moose with characteristic broad, overhanging muzzles, belled throats, and humped shoulders; monarchs of the peaks—mountain goats and the bighorn

sheep; gray wolves, animals enshrined in myths and legends; and mountain lions or pumas, mammals with the greatest natural distribution, aside from humans, in the Western Hemisphere.

The white-tailed deer, a mammal whose white tail is more conspicuous than the rest of its body as it runs away, provides a rare example of a mammal rescued from near extinction. These deer have long been hunted, at first by Indians, then more intensely by European settlers, until the entire species appeared to be in danger of disappearing. Subsequent regulations, management efforts, and environmental changes have stimulated a great increase in their numbers and distribution. In some places, such as the eastern states, this species is more numerous now than it was prior to European colonization.

A black bear with cubs provides the visitor with an endearing sight. These bears breed in June and July, and give birth to one or two tiny, near-naked cubs in the following January or February. The cubs remain denned with their mother until April or May, after which they accompany her until they are yearlings. Since the average female black bear may have two to four litters in her lifetime, each young bear is crucial to her reproductive success.

Like the white-tailed deer and most other related species, the American elk, or wapiti, has been hunted for its meat and antlers, which are sought as trophies. Because the prime bucks yield the most magnificent racks, they are the most favored hunting targets, a practice which in some places has disturbed the usual mating system.

With its Viking helmetlike horn, this African buffalo was among the specimens collected by President Theodore Roosevelt during his 1909–10 African expedition.

Aside from humans, mountain lions or pumas are the mammals with the greatest distribution in the Western Hemisphere.

The white-tailed deer is one of the few large native mammals now more common than it was when North America was first colonized by Europeans.

Above: American elk, or wapiti—a bull, a cow, and a calf—are depicted here migrating down from the high country of Yellowstone National Park after the autumn's first snow. **Bottom photo:** A mother grizzly bear teaches her cubs to dig for ground squirrels near Logan Pass, in Glacier National Park.

Renowned in folklore and in fact for its speed, endurance, and curiosity, the pronghorn is a natural running machine. Its long legs and cloven hooves with shock-absorbing cushions can take it to speeds of 65 miles an hour. Another feature of this antelope is its large eyes set out from the skull, allowing an unusually large field of vision. To top it off, its long black eyelashes serve as sun visors.

The grizzly, or brown bear, in many ways resembles its smaller relative the black bear. The grizzly's vigorous defense of its cubs and search for food often has brought it into conflict with humans. In the short run, it is obvious who usually wins the ensuing battle, but in the long run, the grizzly loses by being systematically wiped out over much of its range.

Last but certainly not least of the large mammals in North America is the bison. Its long, shaggy hair, bearded chin, short upcurving horns, and humped shoulders symbolize the Wild West. Sadly, the bison was pushed to the brink of extinction by meat and hide hunters. Numbers have rebounded in the United States through captive breeding programs, but the only truly wild bison that have survived are in the boggy forests of northwestern Canada and within Yellowstone National Park.

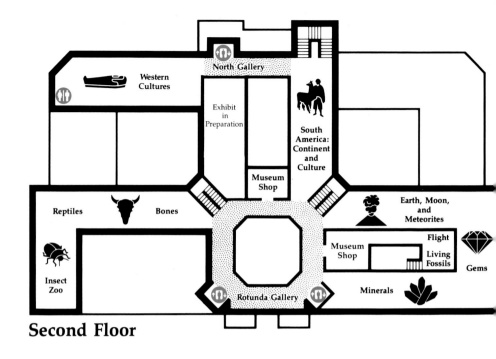

Second Floor

SECOND FLOOR

MINERALS

From the sand underfoot at the beach to the buildings in which we live and work, minerals are an essential part of our daily lives. By definition, a mineral is a naturally occurring inorganic substance having a specific chemical composition and crystal structure. Over 3,500 different types of minerals are arranged systematically according to their chemical composition, with the simplest combinations at the beginning of the hall and the more complex toward the end.

Appropriately, Smithsonite is among the first minerals displayed here. This zinc carbonate, which occurs in various shades—aqua, rose, white, and deep green—was named in honor of the Smithsonian's founder, James Smithson, who identified it.

This Museum has one of the finest, most spectacular accumulations of gold known. The collection features fist-sized nuggets that were panned in America's first "gold rush" in Spotsylvania County, Virginia, and four delicate, leaflike crystal gold pieces found in the 1920s in "California's mother lode."

Many minerals are found as nearly pure metals. Gold, which is native to the United States and is found in other parts of the world, is a good example. Other mineral groups are combinations of elements, including silicates, oxides, carbonates, sulfides, sulfates, halides, and phosphates, representatives of which appear in impressive number throughout the mineral hall. Despite the large number of minerals on display, the exhibited specimens represent only about 3 percent of the total mineral holdings of the Museum, suggesting why its collection is often referred to as the "mecca" of the mineral world.

This exceptionally fine grouping of gypsum crystals came from Mexico. So soft you could scratch it with your fingernail, gypsum is not durable enough to be used as a gemstone.

Considered one of the finest tourmaline specimens in the world, the Candelabra shows the color changes typical of tourmaline crystals. The presence of different impurities during the crystal's growth caused the range of colors.

The Museum's collection of gold nuggets is one of the world's finest.

GEMS

In this hall, some of the finest and most famous precious gems in the world—including diamonds, rubies, sapphires, and emeralds—await you. Among the notable diamonds found in this treasure trove are the 67.89-carat, pear-shaped, Victoria-Transvaal Diamond; the historic Portuguese Diamond, believed to have been found in Brazil; the 235.7-carat Oppenheimer Diamond, the largest uncut, unpolished diamond on display; and the 31-carat, heart-shaped Eugenie Blue Diamond.

Dominating the collection is the most celebrated diamond in the mineral hall—the Hope Diamond. While experts have debunked allegations of a spell or curse associated with the Hope Diamond, its colorful history continues to stoke the fires of intrigue that have contributed to its larger-than-life reputation.

The Hope Diamond's story begins with a reputable French merchant/traveler who in 1642 brought the flawless, 112 3/16-carat, blue diamond out of India and sold it to Louis XIV. Recut to 67 1/8 carats, it became one of the crown jewels of France, set in a magnificent ceremonial piece of jewelry, the Golden

The celebrated Hope Diamond—the best known and largest (45.5 carats) blue diamond in the world—is a centerpiece of the Gems hall.

Although emeralds are the only gems in which imperfections are routinely accepted, the stones in the more than three-century-old Spanish Inquisition Necklace are nearly perfect.

One of a half-dozen rubies in the world large enough and perfect enough to carry an individual name is the 138.7-carat Rosser Reeves Ruby. Another eye-catcher is the Star of Asia Sapphire—a 330-carat blue sapphire, with strong, perfectly defined rays. Star patterns, which may be four- or six-pointed, are created by inclusions running the length of the stones, but the stones have to be cut, polished, and light-oriented for them to appear. If the prism of this stone were cut horizontally, each slice would contain a perfect star. Although emeralds are the only gems in which distracting imperfections are routinely accepted and are referred to as "gardens," the emeralds in the Spanish Inquisition Necklace are nearly perfect.

The dazzling beauty of certain pieces is equalled by their seemingly glamorous histories. For instance, the Empress Marie Louise Tiara was a wedding present commissioned by Napoleon in 1810 for his second wife, the Austrian princess from whom it takes its name. It was originally set with emeralds, but turquoises were substituted later.

A second gift from Napoleon to Empress Marie Louise, the Napoleon Necklace, was made in 1811 and was given in celebration of the birth of the King of Rome. The necklace consists of 28 large round diamonds from which are suspended pendants of briolettes alternating with larger pendants of pear-shaped diamonds: the total carat weight of the diamonds is 275. This necklace is probably the finest piece of Napoleonic jewelry in the United States.

Chinese jade carvings from the 16th–19th centuries, most from the

Fleece. It was stolen in 1792 during the French Revolution and has not been seen since. A 45 1/2-carat blue diamond resurfaced in London 20 years later and is universally believed to have been the French blue diamond recut. It probably was then owned by King George IV of England. Eventually, it came to an American heiress, Evalyn Walsh McLean, who wore it for four decades. After her death, gem dealer Harry Winston bought it and donated it to the Smithsonian. The diamond weighs 45.52 carats and is remarkable for its deep color, rare size, and flawless clarity.

The 1,371-pound "Ring" meteorite, looking like a piece of contemporary sculpture, is one of the many chunks of metal and rock that have fallen to the Earth from outer space and are now in the Museum's collection.

Ching Dynasty (1644–1912), when jade carving reached its peak, close this exhibit area.

EARTH, MOON, AND METEORITES

Meteorites

In 1865, a fire destroyed Smithsonian founder James Smithson's entire 5,000-specimen mineral collection, which included a number of meteorites. Despite this calamitous beginning, the Museum of Natural History has become a national repository for these extraterrestrial visitors from space.

A meteor is a "shooting star," a streak of light across the sky. The object causing that display is a meteoroid, but if that same object reaches the surface of the Earth, it is called a meteorite.

Scientists classify meteorites into three broad groups according to their composition—stone, iron, and stony iron. A map of the United States pinpointing spots where meteorites have been found demonstrates a very uneven distribution, although some meteorites have been found in almost every state. Most are small, but Meteor Crater in northern Arizona was caused by an iron meteorite weighing several hundred thousand tons. An exhibit photograph vividly reveals this 4,000-foot-wide dent in the Earth, which originally was 750 feet deep, and fragments of the original meteorite are on display.

Also on display are more than 150 meteorite specimens of all shapes and sizes, including the 600-pound Clovis meteorite, the largest stony meteorite in the collection, and an eight-pound mate to the missile that crashed through the roof of an Alabama woman's home in 1954, hitting her and severely bruising

One of five moon rocks on display that were collected by Apollo astronauts.

her hip. This is the only known case where a person has been struck by a meteorite.

The collection's most scientifically significant specimen is a remnant of the famous Allende meteorite, which landed in northern Mexico in 1969. Scientists refer to it as a "Rosetta Stone," because it contains material older than the Earth and Moon, making it the oldest mineral specimen ever found and suggesting that it may yield long-concealed secrets about planetary formation.

Today, we know that most meteorites are ancient remnants of the formation of the solar system 4.6 billion years ago. Two theories exist regarding their source—that they are nudged out of an asteroid belt that orbits the Sun between Jupiter and Mars or that they are remnants of dead comets.

Regardless of their source, meteorites have a bearing on the past, present, and future. Some scientists now attribute the sudden extinction of the dinosaurs and large numbers of other living species 65 million years ago to the impact of a giant meteorite that kicked enormous amounts of dust into the atmosphere, thereby blocking sunlight, halting photosynthesis, and disrupting food chains. On a daily basis, more than 50 tons of meteoritic material penetrates our atmosphere, most of it no larger than dust particles. We are now capable of detecting large meteorites on collisional courses with the Earth. In the future it may be possible to develop the technology either to destroy these meteorites in space or to push them into nonthreatening orbits.

Moon

Younger than the meteorites but older than most rocks on Earth, the Moon contains clues to our solar system's origins. Featured here are five lunar samples collected during various Apollo missions, representing the largest collection of lunar materials on display anywhere in the world. A mini-diorama of the Apollo 17 site, complete with the muffled voices of astronauts Harrison Schmitt and Eugene Cernan talking to Robert Parker at Mission Control, injects the drama of discovery into this exhibit area.

Studies of the moon rocks have enabled scientists to divide lunar history into five periods—the Moon's birth 4.6 billion years ago, a molten period 4.6–4.4 billion years ago, an intense meteoritic bombardment period 4.1–3.9 billion years ago, a volcanic period 3.9–3.2 billion years ago, and a quiet Moon from 3.2 billion years ago to the present.

Other exhibits in the hall show the Moon's effects on Earth and trace the changes in man's perception of the Moon over the ages, from the notions expressed in primitive bone scratchings to the precise knowledge gained in the Apollo landings.

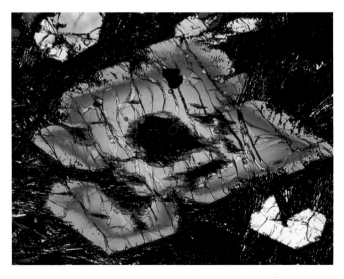

A thin section of one of the moon rocks reveals its mineral content and crystal structure.

This rotating globe, six feet in diameter, presents a "Geologist's View of the Earth."

Earth

If it weren't for the dynamic processes operating on the Earth, its surface would mirror the pockmarked surface of the Moon. While the Earth has suffered many blows from colliding meteorites, most traces of these ancient impacts have been obliterated by weathering erosion, sedimentation, volcanic activity, earth movements, and other geological processes. This hall, with its many geological vignettes, illustrates these processes.

Geologists divide rocks on Earth into three categories: sedimentary, formed at the Earth's surface from the weathering products of pre-existing rocks; igneous, formed by cooling of previously molten material generated deep within the Earth's interior; and metamorphic, formed by the imposition of pressure and/or heat to pre-existing sedimentary or igneous rocks.

Water is the principal agent of sedimentary rock formation, either dissolving minerals and moving the material in solution, or in suspension, as solid particles that settle out in basins of deposition. Today's muds and sands are—with burial, compaction, and dehydration—tomorrow's mudstones and sandstones. The many fossils found elsewhere in this Museum are from sedimentary rock deposits. The erosive qualities of water are exemplified by the large pothole on display.

In igneous rocks, rates of cooling affect rock texture, particularly crystal size. To see a dramatic difference, compare the tiny crystals of a quickly cooled basalt column with the single beryl crystal weighing 980 pounds—the result of a

Nomadic hunters of the South American grasslands, the Tehuelche, throw bolas, weapons that entangle the feet or wings of their prey.

very slow cooling process deep within the Earth.

A globe six feet in diameter offers a geologist's view of our planet, reflecting some of the Earth's long history and the influence of plate tectonics—a concept which holds that the Earth is made up of huge crustal plates that move continually at very slow rates. An orange line on the globe indicates areas where the Earth's crust is splitting and separating.

A mural illustrates the theory of the origins of our solar system.

SOUTH AMERICA

This hall briefly introduces four distinct ecological regions of South America and spans three different time periods—Prehistoric, Colonial, and Modern. By studying the cultures that have adapted to these regions, you can discover how the environment—its resources, soil, and climate—has affected cultural development.

The Grasslands

A life-size diorama of the nomadic Tehuelche Indians riding horseback across the grass-covered Patagonian plains of South America introduces the first region. Armed with bolas—weapons consisting of three rounded weights linked by leather thongs—these Indians are in the midst of a 19th-century hunt. They are throwing a bola at the legs of their prey, the common rhea, a flightless, ostrichlike bird.

Today, this is one of the world's greatest stockraising areas, but the herding of cattle and sheep has replaced the herding of rheas and guanacos, the latter being short-haired relatives of the llama.

Giant tree trunks, branches, vines, and foliage recreate the shrouded rain forest that surrounds the Amazon, one of four ecological regions highlighted in the South America hall.

The Tropical Forest

Upon moving into the heart of the South American continent, the open grasslands fade into the shrouded rain forest surrounding the Amazon, the largest river basin in the world. Giant tree trunks, branches, vines, and foliage, patterned directly from specimens taken from the Amazon forest in Guyana, suggest unbounded fertility, but this is an illusion.

Unlike the case in temperate regions, nutrients here are mostly stored in the plants rather than the soil. Indian tribes such as the Waiwai, who live beneath this lush canopy, solve this problem by abandoning their fields after two or three years. During 50 or more years, soil fertility is gradually restored sufficiently for reuse. Techniques variously known as slash-and-burn, shifting cultivation, or swidden cannot sustain large, permanent settlements. A Waiwai village consists of a single, large, communal house occupied by several related families. On view is the ceremonial dress of these people, including headdresses and nose ornaments made from the brightly colored feathers from male birds of several Amazonian species.

The Mountain Valleys

Although the Amazonians and the Andeans share a boundary, they live in entirely different environments and have developed entirely different ways of life. Amazonian cultures never reached the level of complexity of their highland neighbors, such as Peru, where cities and empires grew, underpinned by food surplus and labor specialization.

At our first stop—the plaza of a mod-

77

This diorama depicts the plaza of a modern Andean town on market day.

ern Andean town on market day—two women, each wearing the clothing typical of her town, are trading vegetables. Potatoes, corn, lima beans, and other crops on sale in this market were domesticated in the Andean highlands long before Inca times and have grown there in abundance ever since.

A replica of a colonial church of 1532 contains various examples of pre-Columbian metalwork, some more than 1,000 years old. Andean peoples had been working metal—including gold, silver, copper, and alloys such as bronze—for over two thousand years at the time of the Spanish conquest.

On the Peruvian coastlands, archeologists have excavated one of the largest prehistoric cities in the Americas—Chan Chan. This planned capital of the great Chimu Empire (A.D. 1200–1470) was supported by a bountiful food supply from irrigated farmlands and the sea. It was dominated by nine large palaces, each over a quarter of a mile long. Fine pottery, gold bracelets, silver tweezers and pins, undoubtedly royal possessions, as well as pottery grave goods are among the articles from the site on view.

The Chimu Empire was conquered by the Incas in 1470. A map showing the extent of the Inca Empire demonstrates that, in less than 100 years after 1438, the Incas conquered territory stretching 2,500 miles and including 10,000 miles of roads. The economy of the Inca Empire was based on surplus production and redistribution of maize and potatoes, foods that still form the basic diet of traditional Andean communities. With an assured food supply, men could be released from the land to serve as soldiers, administrators, and craftsmen, as well as to build roads, temples, fortresses, palaces, and storehouses.

The Arid Coastlands

Fishing helped support large cities along the arid Pacific coastlands. A modern-day Ecuadorian coastal scene caps this South American tour. The centerpiece is a beached balsa raft—over 18 feet long—of a type that fishermen of this area have sailed far out into the Pacific for thousands of years.

The oldest pottery yet found in the New World (3200–1500 B.C.) comes from coastal sites in Ecuador. Called the

Lascaux Cave, France, inhabitated 30,000 years ago by early groups of hunter-gatherers who left behind these cave paintings, is recreated here.

A silver figure, showing a hunchback on a llama (Inca Empire, A.D. 1438–1532), demonstrates the highly sophisticated talents of Andean metallurgists.

Valdivia culture, this pattern is remarkably similar to Japanese pottery of the same time period. In Japan, the style evolved during several millennia, whereas in Ecuador it appears fully developed. Some evidence suggests it was introduced by trans-Pacific voyagers.

ORIGINS OF WESTERN CULTURE
By about 30,000 years ago the pace of human physical evolution had slowed, but the pace of cultural adaptations had accelerated. This exhibit hall, with its more than 2,500 archaeological and ethnographic objects, traces the increasing complexity of culture between the period 20,000 B.C. and 800 A.D. The ancient societies represented strongly influenced the ideas, traditions, and institutions of Western cultures such as those of the United States and Europe.

The Dawn

A recreation of Lascaux Cave in France, which was inhabited by early hunting and gathering groups living during the Late Ice Age—30,000–15,000 years ago— opens this hall. Almost all archaeological remains of these groups that lived in Europe and western Asia relate to hunting, their particular brand of tool manufacture, and various forms of artistic expression, including cave paintings, bone carvings, and sculptures.

Camp to Village

A scene of a herdsman and a partially tamed sheep, both represented by skeletons, dramatizes animal husbandry— one of three crucial processes in human affairs that began in southwest Asia between 9000 and 7000 B.C. The second process, the domestication of wild wheat and barley, required careful scheduling of group movement and storage facilities for the harvest. Animal husbandry and farming combined to trigger the third process—settled life. A diorama based on the mudbrick village of Ali Kosh in southwest Iran contains sickle blades, hoes, and other stone agricultural tools from 7000 B.C., amply demonstrating this transformation. Two adjacent exhibit areas portray the development of two revolutionary technologies—pottery and metallurgy.

From Village to City

About 3500 B.C. the peoples of southern Mesopotamia began to build urban centers. These first cities were supported by the increased food production of commercial agriculture and extensive irrigation, improved technologies such as metallurgy, ranked social classes, and a government bureaucracy. A diorama recreating a scene at the gates of the Mesopotamian city of Larsa in 1801 B.C. highlights some of these changes.

The State

The complexity of urban life that emerged in southwestern Asia before 3000 B.C. fostered a new form of political and social organization called the state, which came to dominate the cultures of Western civilization and which varied in size from the city-state to the unified state to the empire.

The Written Word

Writing developed in response to the needs of the complex commercial and political activities of the city-state. A fascinating collection of cylinder seals, economic tablets and envelopes, clay cones and inscribed bricks demonstrates that the bureaucracy that influenced the lives of the ancient Mesopotamian people may not have differed drastically from today's "red tape."

Ancient Egyptians mummified not only priests and royalty but also embalmed many animals such as this cat, intended to accompany honored human dead to an afterlife in the spirit world.

Egypt

The complex society of ancient Egypt, with its king or pharaoh governing a society of ranked social classes and overseeing a bureaucracy of impressive power, epitomized many of the features associated with the state. The massive tombs and temples along the Nile today are testimonies of a unified government's ability to organize and direct projects requiring thousands of laborers.

Among the many objects in the Egyptian collection are: a funerary stone tablet from 1420 B.C., presented to the United States as a bicentennial gift from Egyptian President Anwar es-Sadat; richly painted coffins from Thebes; mummy masks collected by the great British Egyptologist Sir Flinders Petrie; and mummified hawks, crocodiles, and cats.

This diorama recreates one of two tombs discovered in a Bronze Age (3100 B.C.) cemetery complex at Bab-edh-Dhra, Jordan.

Treasures of Troy

Using clues from Homer's famous epic poems, *The Illiad* and *The Odyssey*, archaeologist Heinrich Schliemann deciphered the location of the ancient city of Troy—at Hissarlik in northwestern Anatolia. More than 100 items from his original excavations there, including beautifully crafted two-handled goblets—Homer's drinking cup of royalty—are on display. This is the only collection of Trojan artifacts in the United States. The collection has assumed added importance because the bulk of the Trojan discoveries, including the great gold treasures, disappeared in Berlin during World War II and has never been recovered.

Other Cultures

A film about the legendary King Gilgamesh; the recreation of two tombs from a Bronze Age (3100 B.C.) cemetery complex at Bab-edh-Dhra, Jordan; and the amazingly complete remains of walled Bronze Age Swiss lake villages (1500–700 B.C.) all provide glimpses of various other cultures. Evidence of cultures flourishing in the Mediterranean from 3000 to 1000 B.C. includes marble figurines from the Cycladic Islands in the Aegean and distinctive pottery decorated with geometric designs from Cyprus and Mycenae. Cultures of the

A bronze Etruscan spirit boat, 1000–500 B.C., which probably served as a lamp, also symbolizes the transport system that linked the peoples of the Mediterranean world.

Elements of classical Greek civilization are revealed in this black-and-red-figure Attic vase.

Roman glass was a major item of trade throughout the empire, and, after the invention of mass production techniques, supplanted pottery for several everyday uses.

Middle East are represented by remarkable bronze objects from Luristan, Iran, and artifacts from Ezion-geber, a coastal settlement between Israel and Jordan, featuring the bronze seal ring of Jotham, one of the ancient kings of Judah.

Trade and Empire
The exchange of products as well as ideas, skills, and information about other people and places opened important lines of communication. Samples of different types of ancient trade goods, both raw materials and manufactured products, piled on a reconstructed dock, form the centerpiece of this section, which also displays ancient inventions, craft techniques, treaties, and business contracts.

Classical Greece
The development of widespread trade networks and subsequent mixing of traditions provided the "raw materials" and economies that fueled the indigenous, rapidly developing cultures of Etruria and Greece. This development, in turn, formed the background for the later culture and civilization of the Roman world.

Black- and red-figure Attic vases from classical Greece reveal many elements of Greek civilization, which was nourished for centuries by the economic, ideological, and military competition between its independent city-states. Some show scenes of and were used at Greek symposia, gatherings where guests reclined on couches, ate elaborate meals, and ostensibly carried on important intellectual discussions. One vase in particular depicts the five contests that made up the pentathlon at the Greek games held in Olympia—long jump, javelin, sprinting, wrestling, and discus throwing.

Rome
Widespread trade networks, protected by the might of the Roman army and administered by the vast Roman bureaucracy, buttressed the Roman Empire. Glass was a major item of trade and, after the invention of mass production techniques, supplanted pottery for several everyday uses. On display is a sampling of ancient glass products.

After the death of Alexander the Great, the Egyptians were ruled first by the Greeks and then by the Romans, during which time Egypt prospered economically and became the intellectual center of the ancient world. Greece and Rome adopted elements of traditional Egyptian culture. A stark reminder of this involves some obvious shortcuts that were later taken with the Egyptian religious tradition of mummifying animals. While the bull mummy on display which would have required considerable effort to prepare, is shaped correctly, X-rays proved it actually contains only a few bull bones and wads of stuffing.

Surviving Traditions
Although the fabric of Western culture has been continuously woven and rewoven through the centuries, basic social and economic patterns persist. In the Near East, the bazaar, or market, has been an essential urban institution since ancient times. Continuities are also reflected in recipes found in a third-century Roman cookbook or the farming hints

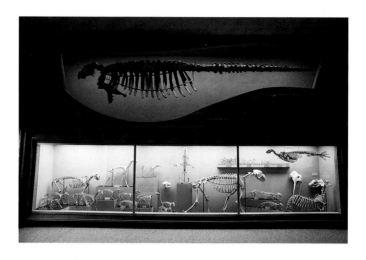

The massive skeleton of a Stellar sea cow—perhaps the most complete such skeleton in existence—looms over skeletons of other meat-eating mammals. It was assembled from bones salvaged on Bering Island in 1883.

offered in an agricultural manual written in the first century A.D.

If you remain skeptical about the endurance of traditions, just look out the window at the classical architectural elements gracing the Interstate Commerce Commission building across the street from the Museum and compare them with the model of the Greek acropolis on display here. Less tangible but equally significant are our theories about government, the organization of the state itself, modern trade practices, and scholarly and literary traditions passed down to us. Contemporary Western civilization culminates in the social developments that stretch back to the end of the Ice Age, to people's first attempts to settle in villages.

BONES

Koalas cling to trees, kangaroos jump, gorillas knuckle-walk, flying lemurs glide, rodents burrow, sea cows paddle, birds and bats fly, snakes crawl, and fish swim, but they couldn't move in any of these marvelous ways without special adaptations within their skeletons.

In this hall, furs, feathers, fins, scales, and skin have been removed, revealing the inside story of hundreds of animals. The skeletons are grouped by taxonomic orders to illustrate their relationships. Fascinating comparisons are evident to the careful viewer. For example, the primate order is illustrated by skeletons of a human, a gorilla, a chimpanzee, and a gibbon.

Exhibits explain how bone is produced, its varying functions, and how bone structures evolved in adaptation to environment. Horses, for example, developed leg and foot bones that enabled them to run swiftly on the level grasslands where they lived and grazed. The skeleton of a famous race horse, Lexington (1850–1875), illustrates this adaptation.

AMPHIBIANS AND REPTILES

Amphibians

Amphibians—the first class of living vertebrates to conquer land—include frogs, salamanders, and the legless caecilians. The word "amphibian," derived from the Greek word "amphibios," meaning double life, sums up some basic characteristics of this group, including their usual life pattern of hatching and developing in water, then undergoing metamorphosis from an aquatic larval stage to a terrestrial or semiaquatic juvenile and adult life. Amphibians are ectotherms, meaning they use the envi-

The American alligator is an integral part of the swamps and marshes of the southeastern United States.

Galapagos marine iguanas, with their crested backs, are the only true sea-living lizards today.

ronment around them to regulate their body temperature. About 300 million years ago, one group of amphibians gave rise to the reptiles.

Reptiles

Modern reptiles—turtles, tuataras, snakes, crocodiles, and lizards—are also ectotherms. All are covered with scales and early in their evolution developed a terrestrial egg to become independent of water for reproduction. A Florida Everglades scene contains the American alligator, an integral part of the swamps and marshes of the southeastern United States. Many animals depend upon 'gator holes for survival during the unpredictable recurring droughts.

Of special interest is the Komodo monitor, or "dragon," the largest living lizard, reaching more than 365 pounds. This particular specimen was brought to the museum after it died of old age at the Smithsonian's National Zoo in the 1970s. Its "septic tank" mouth is filled with putrescent bacteria, a condition the Komodo dragon exploits when capturing prey, such as deer or pigs. The Ko-

A tarantula sits in the palm of a hand. A schedule of the ever-popular tarantula feeding is posted at the Insect Zoo.

modo dragon typically wages a surprise attack, biting its victim on the abdomen or legs, inflicting septicemia, or blood poisoning, in the process. The prey may initially escape, but does not travel far before lying down and dying. The lizard then finds it by smell, often sharing it with other dragons.

Galapagos marine iguanas, with their crested backs, are the only true sea-living lizards today. They feed exclusively underwater on tidal and subtidal algae. When up on rocks, their black bodies rapidly absorb heat, and elevated body temperatures speed digestion. The Galapagos Islands have many strange and wonderful animals and plants. Indeed, the diversity of these organisms and their patterns of similarities and differences from island to island led Charles Darwin to the development of the theory of evolution by natural selection. While aspects of this theory have changed, the basic concept of natural selection (differential reproduction and survival) remains the core of evolutionary theory and thought today.

THE O. ORKIN INSECT ZOO

Insects and their relatives are the world's most successful inhabitants. In both number and kind, there are more arthropods than any other animals. Scientists estimate that this phylum of invertebrates may account for up to 99 percent of animal species. In the new Insect Zoo, live displays, interactive exhibits, and simulated habitats show how arthropods are "Designed for Survival."

The Amazing Arthropods

Visitors enter the exhibit through an archway filled with insect specimens and are immediately surrounded by a sea of insects and their songs. On one wall lighted clusters of pinned specimens show the sheer diversity of form. On another a diorama of giant primitive insects portrays life in the Carboniferous

A leaf-cutter ant exhibits the technique that earned it its name.

period, 350 million years ago, when arthropods were beginning to diversify and spread over the land. Live examples illustrate each of the five major arthropod classes—insects, arachnids, millipedes, centipedes, and crustaceans.

Thriving through Change
Adaptability is one important key to insects' great success in finding food and reproducing. Special mouth structures enable different insects to eat different foods—plants, meat, or both. Long antennae help plant-eaters such as katydids pick up the scent of food, while large eyes enable meat-eaters such as dragonflies to spot flies and mosquitoes. Thanks to short breeding cycles and a variety of developmental processes, many insects can reproduce quickly and in great numbers. And flying provides them with more places to search for food—as well as a way to escape danger.

Dealing with Danger
Surrounded by enemies larger than themselves, insects have evolved appearances that serve as defensive weapons. Some protect themselves by camouflage with their surroundings or by resemblance to inedible objects. Others avoid being eaten by mimicking the appearance of distasteful or dangerous species, or by using bright colors to startle and confuse predators.

Insect Societies
Some small insects survive by banding together in highly organized groups to share housing, care of the young, work, food, and protection. A full-size, crawl-through replica of an African termite mound—the pinnacle of insect engineering—has cut-away walls to expose the interior nest structure. Built-in video monitors capture the teeming metropolis at work. Other displays show how honeypot ants, Costa Rican acacia ants, and termites cooperate.

Habitats
No other group of animals can match the wide range of habitats arthropods occupy. Recreations of several contrasting habitats reveal how insects and their

The treehopper, looking like a "thorn" with eyes, may trick its enemies with its prickly appearance.

relatives have adapted to diverse and far-flung surroundings and carved out a tremendous variety of niches. A desert habitat looks at ways desert arthropods are modified to survive heat, water shortages, and evaporation. A freshwater habitat shows how ponds offer insects as many different living spaces as land. A mangrove habitat features arthropods that can adapt to constantly changing temperatures and water salinity. And a walk-through tropical rainforest bursts with life, including insects filling many different niches—ground litter, tree trunk nooks and crannies, water-filled bromeliad plants, dark caves, and the upper reaches of the forest canopy.

Our House, Their House
Humans have unwittingly created a perfect, year-round tropical setting for insects. A re-creation of a typical home and yard acquaints visitors with uninvited guests they may come in contact with but know little about—clothes moths, roaches, silverfish, flies, carpenter ants, mosquitoes, and fireflies. An interactive game focuses on the array of benefits insects provide such as honey, silk, pollination, and decomposition. A replication of a tree hollow with a real honeybee hive allows visitors to observe bees bringing pollen and nectar into the hive through a plexiglass tube connected to the outdoors.

Entomologists at Work
Through a window in the Insect Zoo rearing room, visitors can view staff scientists at work as well as technicians feeding and caring for colonies of live specimens used for displays. The changing exhibit area "Scientist's Corner" highlights research projects of Smithsonian entomologists.

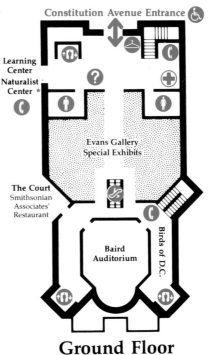

Ground Floor

GROUND FLOOR

CONSTITUTION AVENUE ENTRANCE

Learning Center

Naturalist Center

Evans Gallery
Special Exhibits

The Court
Smithsonian
Associates'
Restaurant

Baird
Auditorium

Birds of D.C.

The exhibit Birds of the District of Columbia Region *features the avian inhabitants of an area extending from the Atlantic Ocean to the Allegheny Mountains—including this northern goshawk, a very rare winter visitor, with its victim, a bluejay, at its feet.*

GROUND FLOOR

CONSTITUTION AVENUE LOBBY
An exhibit of 250 splendors from every scientific department gives visitors a taste of what they can see in the Museum. Major objects of interest include a fossil tooth from a 45-foot shark, a bird's nest turned to calcite, a nearly 1-million-year-old hand ax from Kenya, brilliantly-colored Morpho butterflies, Pueblo pottery by Maria Martinez, Burgess shale fossils, meteorites, and a 70-million-year-old dinosaur skull. One changing display features recent acquisitions to the Museum's collection; another highlights research carried out by Museum scientists. And 35-foot totem poles dominate a display on historical and contemporary art of Northwest Coast Native Americans.

BIRDS OF THE DISTRICT OF COLUMBIA
An 1829 engraving of an original watercolor by John James Audubon of a swal-

The Naturalist Center invites the public to study its natural history collections, housed in storage cases similar to those in the Museum's research areas.

low-tailed kite marks the entrance to this exhibit, located in the curved hallway encircling the Baird Auditorium. Almost 300 mounted species representative of the birds of eastern United States are shown here, including some superb examples of hawks and eagles.

NATURALIST CENTER
At the Naturalist Center anyone can have the experience of studying actual natural history specimens firsthand. The collection of more than 28,000 natural history items includes rocks, bottles with marine organisms, mounted insects, stone Indian artifacts, plant specimens, bird skins, and animal skeletons. Visitors may also use scientific instruments, consult books and references, view videotapes, or follow self-learning guides.

The Center represents a bridge between the relatively few, largely untouchable display specimens in the exhibits and the millions of hands-on research collections in storage behind the scenes. It is divided into six areas (anthropology, plants, invertebrates, vertebrates, minerals and rocks, and fossils) representing scientific disciplines covered in the Museum as a whole. The Center gives the scientifically curious a chance to conduct rock identification experiments, compare a normal human bone with one grazed by a bullet or attacked by a disease, study a dried plant, feel the downy softness of a hummingbird nest, or hold a Triceratops horn unearthed from the Age of Reptiles.

Samples of the natural and cultural treasures found throughout the Museum bring the North Foyer to life.

An osteologist and Museum technician study a bird feather under a scanning electron microscope, which magnifies the feather hundreds of times.

BEYOND THE EXHIBITS

For most visitors, the National Museum of Natural History/National Museum of Man conjures up one image—that of the public exhibition halls, where a small portion of the Museum's vast holdings are arrayed in informative, artistic displays. Few of the visiting millions are aware of the larger collections from which these exhibits are drawn, or that the exhibits represent the tip of an iceberg—the end result of a long process of discovery, acquisition, preparation, study, curation, interpretation, and finally display.

Any full tour of the National Museum of Natural History/National Museum of Man, if such were possible, would take the visitor on a far lengthier trek than even the most exhaustive study of the Museum's exhibit halls. Such a tour would proceed from the second floor galleries to the third and fourth floors, and beyond the main building into the vast hallways of the East and West wings, where there are no public exhibits at all. Here in the offices, laboratories, libraries, and storage areas, more than 1,000 people work—the scientists, computer specialists, technicians, conservators, librarians, scientific illustrators, photographers, education and information specialists, fossil preparators, and numerous others carrying on the vital work of the Museum. In laboratories from basement to attic and out in the field on several continents, Museum scientists work to advance knowledge of the natural world.

A Smithsonian botanist collects unusual plants on an isolated mountain in Amazonas, Venezuela.

A marine biologist studies sponges under a microscope at the Museum's Carrie Bow Cay research station.

If you were to take a tour behind the scenes, you might see volunteers piecing together shards of a Palestinian pot; technicians slicing thin sections of bones or rocks for physical anthropologists or geologists to study; a scientific illustrator putting the final touches on a detailed drawing of a newly discovered species of spider; a botanist preparing a paper on plant evolution that she will give at an upcoming international symposium; an archaeologist mapping the artifacts discovered in an excavation in Colorado; a preparator using dental picks to release an extinct animal from its tomb of stone; a biologist preparing a description of a new species of shrimp discovered on a recent expedition to the Indian Ocean; or a conservator sewing a delicate Eskimo gutskin parka for an upcoming exhibit.

A full tour would include still more. You would, indeed, have to go into the field, accompanying one of the scientists engaged in the process of discovery. Whether on a remote island in the Indian Ocean or at the Museum's marine station in Florida, whether in a small vil-

Museum archaeologists excavate a 6,000-year-old settlement site in Labrador.

lage in Africa or Mexico or a remote corner of Tibet, whether in the depths of the Pacific Ocean or in the ancient hills of Pakistan, the coral reefs of Belize, the coast of Labrador, the rain forest of Brazil, or the volcanoes of Hawaii, you could find museum scientists discovering new species and new habitats, uncovering new artistic expressions or archaeological sites, explaining geological processes through new techniques or theories, and otherwise fitting together new pieces in the enormous puzzle of the history and diversity of life and human culture on our planet.

A Carabid beetle from the museum's collections, precisely drawn by senior scientific illustrator George Venable, symbolizes the Museum's dedication to the study, understanding, and conservation of the natural world.

POPULAR EXHIBITS

The National Museum of Natural History contains many intriguing and fascinating objects. Some of the most popular exhibits are listed below in the order that they appear in this guidebook and with their locations in parentheses.

African bush elephant and Bengal tiger (Rotunda—first floor)

Murchison meteorite, thought to be a remnant of the birth of the Universe (Earliest Traces of Life—first floor)

Earliest ancestor yet known of all life forms on Earth (Earliest Traces of Life—first floor)

Shark! the reconstructed jaw of the biggest shark that ever lived (balcony—second floor)

92-foot-long blue whale model (Marine Ecosystems—first floor)

Coral Reef and Maine Coast Aquaria (Marine Ecosystems—first floor)

Gold nuggets panned in America's first gold rush (Minerals—second floor)

Hope Diamond (Gems—second floor)

Moon rocks collected on Apollo missions (Earth, Moon, and Meteorites—second floor)

Treasures from Egypt, Troy, Greece, Rome (Origins of Western Culture—second floor)

Naturalist Center with hands-on natural history study collections (ground floor)

Especially for Children
If you are touring the Museum with young children and have only a couple of hours, the following exhibits may be of interest:

Diplodocus longus (Dinosaurs—first floor)

Life-size model of a pterosaur (Flight, balcony—second floor)

Mammoth, mastodon, and giant ground sloth (Ice Age Mammals—first floor)

Kathakali dancer (Asian Cultures—first floor)

Toys from India, Pakistan, and China (Asian Cultures—first floor)

Discovery Room, where visitors of all ages can see, touch, smell, and taste a variety of natural history specimens (first floor)

Insect Zoo, including its glass beehive (second floor)

GENERAL INFORMATION

Continued from front cover

other museum-related objects are also for sale. A smaller shop is located on the second floor.

Special Exhibitions Special temporary exhibitions, either on loan or organized by the Smithsonian, are installed in the large Thomas M. Evans Gallery on the ground floor or the Rotunda Gallery on the second floor.

Naturalist Center The Naturalist Center houses collections that amateur naturalists may touch, examine, and study. Materials may be brought to the Center for identification. Children age 12 and above are permitted, but must be accompanied by an adult. Groups of five or more must make advance reservations. For an application, call (202) 357-2747, TTY (202) 357-1696.

Discovery Room Visitors of all ages may see, touch, feel, and smell a variety of natural history specimens. The Discovery Room is open Monday through Thursday from 12:00 noon to 2:30 p.m.; Friday through Sunday from 10:30 a.m. to 3:30 p.m., except some holidays. Groups of five or more must make advance reservations; for an application, call (202) 357-2747; TTY (202) 357-1696. Free tickets, which can be obtained at the first floor Rotunda information desk, are required on weekends and some holidays.

Visitors with Disabilities A ramp is located at the Constitution Avenue entrance. All exhibits and restrooms are fully accessible. For information on the services available for visitors with disabilities, call Smithsonian Information at (202) 357-2700; TTY 357-1729.

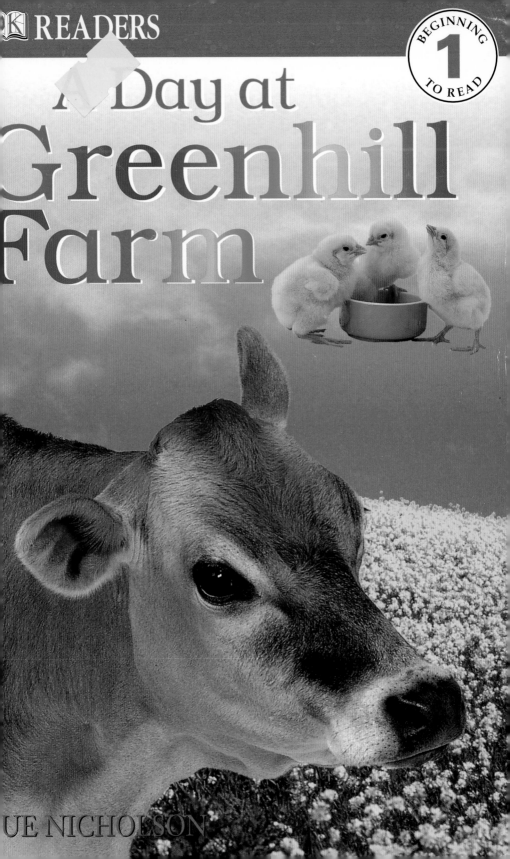

DK Readers

A Day at Greenhill Farm

UE NICHOLSON

𝕯𝕶 READERS

Level 1

A Day at Greenhill Farm
Truck Trouble
Tale of a Tadpole
Surprise Puppy!
Duckling Days
A Day at Seagull Beach
Whatever the Weather
Busy Buzzy Bee
Big Machines
Wild Baby Animals
A Bed for the Winter
Born to be a Butterfly
Dinosaur's Day
Feeding Time
Diving Dolphin
Rockets and Spaceships
My Cat's Secret
First Day at Gymnastics
A Trip to the Zoo
I Can Swim!
A Trip to the Library

A Trip to the Doctor
A Trip to the Dentist
I Want To Be A Ballerina
Animal Hide and Seek
Submarines and Submersibles
Animals at Home
Let's Play Soccer
LEGO: Trouble at the Bridge
LEGO: Secret at Dolphin Bay
Star Wars: What is a Wookiee?
Star Wars: Ready, Set, Podrace!
A Day in the Life of a Builder
A Day in the Life of a Dancer
A Day in the Life of a Firefighter
A Day in the Life of a Teacher
A Day in the Life of a Musician
A Day in the Life of a Doctor
A Day in the Life of a Police Officer
A Day in the Life of a TV Reporter
Gigantes de Hierro *en español*
Crías del mundo animal *en español*

Level 2

Dinosaur Dinners
Fire Fighter!
Bugs! Bugs! Bugs!
Slinky, Scaly Snakes!
Animal Hospital
The Little Ballerina
Munching, Crunching, Sniffing,
   and Snooping
The Secret Life of Trees
Winking, Blinking, Wiggling,
   and Waggling
Astronaut: Living in Space
Twisters!
Holiday! Celebration Days
   around the World
The Story of Pocahontas
Horse Show
Survivors: The Night the Titanic Sank
Eruption! The Story of Volcanoes
The Story of Columbus
Journey of a Humpback Whale
Amazing Buildings
Feathers, Flippers, and Feet

Outback Adventure: Australian
   Vacation
Sniffles, Sneezes, Hiccups, and Coughs
Ice Skating Stars
Let's Go Riding
I Want to Be a Gymnast
Starry Sky
Earth Smart: How to Take Care
   of the Environment
Water Everywhere
Telling Time
A Trip to the Theater
LEGO: Castle Under Attack
LEGO: Rocket Rescue
Star Wars: Journey Through Space
Star Wars: A Queen's Diary
MLB: A Batboy's Day
MLB: Let's Go to the Ballpark!
Spider-Man: Worst Enemies
Meet the X-Men
¡Insectos! *en español*
¡Bomberos! *en español*
La Historia de Pocahontas *en español*